Sacred

Pampering Principles

Sacred
Pampering
Principles

AN AFRICAN-AMERICAN WOMAN'S
GUIDE TO SELF-CARE AND INNER RENEWAL

Debrena Jackson Gandy

William Morrow and Company, Inc. ● *New York*

It is the policy of William Morrow and Company, Inc., and its imprints and affiliates, recognizing the importance of preserving what has been written, to print the books we publish on acid-free paper, and we exert our best efforts to that end.

Gandy, Debrena Jackson.
    Sacred pampering principles : an African-American woman's guide to self-care and inner renewal / Debrena Jackson Gandy.
        p.   cm.
    ISBN 0-688-14751-8
    1. Afro-American women—Religious life.   2. Afro-American women—Conduct of life.   I. Title.
    BL625.2.G36   1997
    158'.1'082—dc20   96-27808
                                                                        CIP

Printed in the United States of America

First Edition

1   2   3   4   5   6   7   8   9   10

BOOK DESIGN BY LEAH S. CARLSON

To my little girls, Adera and Kiana,
and the future pampered women of the world

ACKNOWLEDGMENTS

Writing this book has shown me how much of a spiritual process writing can be. I am very clear that this book came *through* me, not from me. Many thanks to the incredible people and divine circumstances that played a part in the birth of this project. Special thanks to:

Nat and Thelma Jackson, Mama and Daddy, for being the conduits that brought me into this world;

Ericka, my loving sister, for being the critical link in the series of divine connections that brought this book about;

"Little J," my brilliant little brother, for helping me when I couldn't figure out how to get my computer to work;

Adera and Kiana, my little girls, for their warm hugs while I was typing the book manuscript, and their assistance pulling the finished pages off of my laser printer;

Iyanla Vanzant, for so graciously introducing this project idea to her literary agent;

My sisterfriends for their ongoing cheerleading and authentic support;

Denise Stinson, for being the literary agent par excellence;

Will Schwalbe and Doris Cooper of William Morrow and Company, Inc., for being the "bestest" editorial team in the world;

Joseph Gandy, my husband, best friend, and pampering partner;

And to God/Goddess, for allowing me to be on this planet at this time sharing this very necessary message.

CONTENTS

Sacred

Pampering Principles

INTRODUCTION: GET READY, GET SET

My mom, whom I adoringly call Mama, gave me some of my first examples of pampering. A regular part of Mama's pampering regime was a trip to the beauty salon to get her hair done every three weeks. Rain, shine, sleet, or snow. Like clockwork. The same beauty salon, the same beautician. For the past twenty-five years. It was an opportunity for her to connect and bond with other women through the exchanges of common stories and "Yeah, girl" shoptalk and advice. It was her opportunity to sit back and be served as her hair was shampooed and agile fingers massaged her scalp.

And Mama was definitely not a shower woman, she was a bath woman. She kept her colorful assortment of bath-bubble bottles sitting along the back edge of the bathtub. There were *our* bath bubbles, and then there were Mama's. And my sister and I knew not to get the two confused. When Mama was taking one of her pampering bubble baths, which she called a soak, my sister and I knew not to knock on the bathroom door with any of our creative interruptions, such as claiming that we were in a "tight" and had to go "pee."

Then there was Mama's signature perfume, Emeraude, in its familiar tall light-green bottle. She kept a supply of Emeraude perfume, lotion, *and* body powder, complete with its big, round, fluffy powder puff, on her dresser. And on Sunday mornings when it was time to "lotion up," she'd remind my sister and me never to forget our knees, heels, and elbows. She'd tell us that a woman should always take time to lotion her body so that she wasn't "ashy." On those rare occasions when she ran out of her Emeraude lotion, she always had her faithful backup. The tall yellow pump bottle of Vaseline Intensive Care lotion would serve as a temporary substitute until she could replenish her Emeraude supply.

Or there was Mama's quarter-acre garden, famous throughout Thurston County for the luscious, oversized vegetables it produced. As a little girl I didn't understand why Mama so thoroughly enjoyed digging in the dirt, pulling weeds, and suffering the calluses and cracked hands that were the by-products of her devoted gardening. At that time in my life I didn't have the insight and maturity to recognize that Mama was doing much more than tilling the soil, pulling weeds, and planting seeds—she was an artist at work. In the process of nurturing and cultivating those little seeds, Mama was also pampering herself—rejuvenating her mind, body, and spirit.

For Mama gardening was a seasonal ritual that she anticipated with as much excitement as a little girl on the night before Christmas. I watched her ritual progress and unfold as she lovingly reaped the "fruits of her labor"—yellow crookneck squash, collard greens, zucchini, carrots, onions, peppers, and tomatoes. She then transformed her harvest into delicious homemade creations like zucchini bread, carrot-walnut cake, vegetable stir-fry, canned chow-chow relish, or a pot of tasty collard greens.

As she put her hands into that rich dark soil season after season, she became a co-creator with Mother Earth. A motto carved into a small wooden plaque that sits in the corner of her garden says, "Who plants a seed beneath the sod, And waits to see believes in God." This practice of tilling, fertilizing, planting, weeding, and watering was far more than just gardening; she was engaged in a ritual that brought her immense joy and pleasure. She was pampering herself.

Years later, once I graduated from college, my aunt, Priscilla, became a pampering role model who opened up new dimensions of pampering to me. When I was a freshman in college, I spent a weekend in Los Angeles with Aunt Priscilla, whom I hadn't seen since I was a little girl. My cousin picked me up at Pepperdine and we drove into Los Angeles. During the forty-five-minute drive into Los Angeles from Malibu, I was both nervous and anxious since I hadn't seen Aunt Priscilla in over fifteen years. Would we get along? What would she be like now? What did she look like?

As soon as I walked into her house, my worries evaporated. I was enveloped by a sense of comfort and warmth. Her home was decorated with soothing colors, elegant silk-flower arrangements, and lovely framed pictures of African-American art. I felt comfortable and at home right away. Aunt Priscilla came out of her bedroom and greeted me with a welcoming smile and warm hug. I thought to myself, *Wow, she's beautiful.* She had that classic Lena Horne type of beauty—vibrant, elegant, shapely, striking features, and looking years younger than her actual age. She showed me where to put my suitcase and then invited me back to her bedroom to watch some TV and get caught up on life. The TV, however, was my least concern. I was fascinated with my aunt, and I wanted to sop up all of her that I could while I was here for the weekend.

The decor and the arrangement of her bedroom suggested that it was much more than just a place to sleep—it looked and felt like an inviting personal sanctuary. The soft, plush carpet was coordinated with the pastel theme of the bedspread and curtains. A stationary exercise bike was positioned in the corner. An easy chair was snuggled in the corner near the door. And she had adjusted a dimmer switch to give the room a soft glow. All of these were new bedroom concepts to me. I had seen pictures of these types of fancy bedroom setups in furniture catalogs, but not in real life. Yes, this was more than just a bedroom, this was my aunt's personal refuge.

As we continued to get caught up on the details of my freshman college experience, she began to paint her toenails. The toenail painting itself wasn't such a big deal. It was *how* she painted them. She gently stuck small balls of cotton between each toe so that the polish wouldn't smudge while it dried, and painted each nail with the utmost grace and loving care, as if each toe were a precious jewel.

Now, I was used to quickie toenail painting jobs—whipping out the nail polish, hurriedly slapping a few strokes over a chipped coat, and dashing out the door. Not the unrushed, deliberate process my aunt was demonstrating. She was painting her toes as if it was the most important labor of love in the world. I asked her about this meticulous toe-painting business and she replied, "It's important for a woman to take good care of her body, it's the only one she's got." She went on, "But this requires that you slow down and take

the time to treat your body lovingly, like it's a precious temple."
This "treat your body like a temple" concept was both new and
intriguing to me. Looking at my aunt, it was obvious that it worked.

Pause and reflect for a moment. Who in your life provided you
with some of your first living examples of pampering? Was it your
mother? An aunt? An older sister? Your grandmother or a neigh-
bor? Pampering is not new to Black women, we just need to jog
our cellular memory, to remember. We have to return to living
lives where balance is highly valued and we see spiritual renewal as
essential to our well-being.

Our legacy of finding a way to pamper ourselves in spite of the
odds stretches far back to advanced civilizations, such as ancient
Egypt, which Black people spawned. Ancient cultural pampering
practices could include a woman retreating to spend sacred time
with other women during her menses; women oiling their bodies
with precious scented oils to keep their skin soft and supple; giving
themselves facials with the mud from the Nile to help draw out
impurities in their skin; bonding with one another by lovingly
braiding each other's hair; or using herbal plant extracts to heal
and soothe their bodies.

The Bible contains many examples of pampering. For example
Proverbs 7:17 speaks of a woman perfuming her bed with myrrh,
aloe, and cinnamon. And Proverbs 27:9 says that "ointment and
perfume rejoice the heart." In biblical times fragrant substances
were exotic and highly valued.

Throughout the ages, as Black women, we have managed to
find creative ways to pamper ourselves even when conditions were

tough and the going was rough. Whether it was "front-porch ther-apy" such as the rhythmic poppin' of snap beans, stemmin' greens, or shellin' peas on the front porch, or the calming repetition of braiding each other's hair, we found ways to convert necessary work into practices that could bring us back to our center, keep us sane when we were on edge, calm frazzled nerves, and renew a tired soul.

One of the glorious things about pampering, just as with other transformational, life-changing practices, is that it has the unique distinction of simultaneously being the means *and* the end, the pro-cess *and* the outcome, the destination and the journey. Pampering helps you relate to yourself in a new and different way—a way in which care of self is a top priority. And a priority that doesn't arise out of selfishness but arises out of a place of healthy self-love and self-support. Pampering is at once a path to greater self-love and self-discovery *and* an active demonstration of self-love.

Pampering is not self-serving, it's conscious self-service.

This is why embracing a new paradigm of self-care and inner re-newal is so necessary for us right now, especially as we move into the new millennium. Black women need collectively to shift to a *new place* that allows us to claim our right to love, joy, passion, and pleasure instead of struggle, obligation, and effort. In this new place personal well-being is primary, not secondary to everything and everyone else. Our health and well-being depend on us making this shift. *Our lives depend on it.*

Pampering is not about adding more things to the "to do" list of your already full life. Pampering is about making a shift to integrating experiences and making more choices in your life that bring you joy, peace, and pleasure. These shifts in mind-set and deep-seated beliefs *show up* in your life and are reflected in your actions and behaviors, and in how you treat *yourself* tri-dimensionally—mind, body, and spirit. These shifts can impact your entire life: your self-image, love relationships, body, appearance, friendships, marriage, interactions with your children, energy level, productivity, and sex life. Simply put, pampering is orienting your life around what brings you joy.

1

THE SBW SYNDROME

I think our obsession with "busyness," overdoing it, overworking, overextending ourselves, and overnurturing others—that is, the Strong Black Woman (SBW) Syndrome—is a haunting remnant of the powerful Mammie and Aunt Jemima images that are still anchored deeply in our minds from slavery. The SBW Syndrome has an insidious way of pervading our lives, shaping our beliefs and thus our behaviors, attitudes, and actions. These images are then reinforced by society, the media, and cultural conditioning.

Mammie was the nurturer, "the omnipotent caregiver," the always-listening ear, the "everlasting arm." Mammie provided the shoulder for everybody else to lean on. She was the Rock of Gibraltar, the Strong Black Woman who constantly gave out love, attention, and affection but who didn't ask for it, appear to need it, or require it in return. She could give, give, give, and do, do, do without seeming to need a break, a breather, or a vacation.

Other ways the SBW Syndrome shows up is when we become control freaks and micromanagers of almost everything and everyone in our lives. In turn, others in our lives respond in ways that perpetuate and reinforce the syndrome. We have a tendency to take over or dominate, and in turn others *let* us, and even come to expect it. They figure we can handle it.

We have a hard time delegating and trusting that it will be done right or get done at all—then we end up doing it ourselves, once again. We start feeling stressed out and depleted. The Syndrome can creep in and quietly start to show up at work, at home, and in our relationships. We look up and others have become too dependent on us. Over time we start to become resentful because we don't feel we're getting the support we need. We start to feel others are not pulling their share of the load. But what we often don't realize is that we've been instrumental in creating the very situation that has us so frustrated.

In *Sisters of the Yam: black women and self-recovery*, bell hooks explains her realization about the connection between personal power and self-care. She writes,

> *Since many black women (myself included) allow ourselves to become overextended—working, meeting the needs of others—we often do not take time for care of the self. And those among us who have been socialized from childhood on to feel that black women's "personal power" only comes through serving others may have the most difficult time learning to see that personal power really begins with care of the self.*

Self-care is empowering, plain and simple. The SBW Syndrome can have you feeling like you're in a trap, suffering quietly, but you can't figure out how to undo the lock. *Sacred Pampering Principles* offers you a key.

As Black women this approach to doing life is not entirely self-created, however. We acquired it from our mothers, who acquired it from *their* mothers. This syndrome has been passed down through the generations. The circumstances and environment of our mothers and grandmothers often necessitated it, but ours doesn't have to.

This approach to life that many of us have "inherited" brings to mind the image of a pole that I call our Priority Pole. The Priority Pole represents the hierarchy of things and people in our lives. Unfortunately the bottom slot on the Priority Pole is the spot many of us have reserved for ourselves in relation to our other life priorities—family, career, relationships, community, church, and friends. *We give our best to everyone and everything else and then leave only the "slim pickin's" and "leftovers" for ourselves.* We ensure that everyone else above us on our Priority Pole is cared for, considered, included, comfortable, nurtured, and accommodated FIRST, *then* we see to our own needs—often last *and* least. This Bottom-of-the-Priority-Pole mentality and posture we tend to take on in life is also a complex combination of media conditioning, namely TV and movie images, family conditioning, mirroring behaviors we saw older females in our families exhibit, our moms especially, as our very first mother-wife-parent-caregiver role models.

The SBW Syndrome has the effect of wedging us into a definition and a role that doesn't allow for us fully to receive affection, assistance, love, nurturing, and support. It negates our femininity. A big part of what keeps us in the trap is the low priority we give ourselves, our bodies, and our needs. As we grow up, we silently draw conclusions about where and how we fit in—and the *bottom* of the Priority Pole is the place we carve out for ourselves and our mental, physical, emotional, and spiritual needs. This self-sacrificing, Bottom-of-the-Priority-Pole mentality is not only unhealthy, it undermines our personal power, well-being, energy, and self-worth.

SETTING THE STAGE

Many of us are at the point where we are flat out overwhelmed and overextended. We're giving way too much without expecting, requesting, or allowing for reciprocity. We are overaccommodating and overnurturing others at a serious personal expense. Many of us have had enough. We're about to pull our hair out because we can't figure out how to slow life down to let us off so that we can take a break. We want to disentangle ourselves from the sticky tentacles of this trap of doing everything for everybody else at the expense of our own needs, but we don't know how or where to begin. If you have been feeling like you're standing on quicksand, *Sacred Pampering Principles* is designed to help you find firm footing. *Sacred Pampering Principles* can help you get out of this potentially overwhelming and suffocating predicament.

We're in *pursuit*—of happiness, of Mr. Right, of a raise, of peace of mind, of the almighty dollar, and of satisfaction and "full-fill-ment." We've been led to think that "busyness" leads to greater fulfillment. It seems we're obsessed with the *pursuit*, but the rat race has lost its thrill. Being in pursuit just isn't cutting it anymore. We strive to make more money so that we can buy a newer car or get a bigger house. And then we have to work harder to earn the money so that we can continue to cover the expense of the newer car and the bigger house. This cycle is insane. Then when we stop for a moment to lift our noses from the grindstone, we ask *Why am I still so unfulfilled and dissatisfied?*

Sacred Pampering Principles can free you from the bondage of both the SBW Syndrome and the Pursuit Obsession. First, it is a tool to help you identify and recognize the deep-seated beliefs, attitudes, values, and behaviors that keep you in the trap. Second, it will help you get back in touch with what brings you joy and pleasure in life. Third, it will give you some gentle guidelines, processes, and prescriptions to help you bring your life into balance. And fourth, it will assist you in maintaining a lifestyle integrated with pampering, a lifestyle in which joy and pleasure are no longer pursued but are an integral part of your daily life experience. After all, pampering is not a self-only approach to life, it a *self-care-first* approach.

So What Exactly Is Pampering?

When I started speaking on the subject of pampering and self-care several years ago, early on I realized that my definition of pampering and others' definition of pampering were very different. Time and again I'd ask Black women how they defined pampering, and the initial response invariably was "getting my nails done or getting my hair done." I quickly came to realize that there were some important distinctions I needed to make when it came to *my* functional definition of pampering. To me what women were describing as pampering was what I considered to be grooming.

Black women do a lot of grooming. Grooming, however, is an

"outside" job. Grooming alone has a very marginal effect on our inner joy. Grooming is external, primarily physical and tends to focus on improving our "packaging," our outer appearance. You may *look* good but not *feel* good. Your nails may be slammin', your makeup flawless, your hair whipped, and your outfit well coordinated, but emotionally, mentally, and spiritually you can feel empty and depleted.

Pampering, on the other hand, is an "inside" job, *inner* grooming so to speak. It refuels and recharges your mind, body, and spirit and infuses your life with more joy. Pampering's focus is always brought back to the *inner* self. And in turn, pampering transforms your outer self. Pampering taps you into the essence of your personal joy, not culturally or socially dictated or determined but *personally* defined.

To keep us crystal clear about what qualifies as pampering, I'd like to share the three criteria for pampering that must be achieved *simultaneously,* not one or two in isolation of the other, to be doing what I call pampering:

1. The experience is one in which *you* are the primary beneficiary.
2. The experience brings you joy and increases your inner peace.
3. The experience nurtures your body, mind, and spirit.

Let me explain in greater detail why these three particular criteria were chosen and why they must be achieved *together.*

As women we are very good at forgoing or compromising our

needs so that others can be happy or comfortable. Often the closest we get to directly experiencing *personal* joy is through someone else. Pampering is intended to be, first, a direct experience of *your* choosing where *your* joy, inner renewal, and peace of mind are the primary objectives. Thus you being the primary beneficiary is an essential first criteria for pampering. You have to be lovingly reminded that personal pampering is uniquely for *you*—not for you and the kids, not for you and your man, not for you and your friends.

Second, a pampering experience is one that *brings you joy*. Pampering experiences are joy-focused and joy-centered. Notice that the second criterion says "brings you joy" in contrast to "makes you happy." This is a crucial distinction.

Something that "makes you happy" *causes* you to become pleased. In our Western culture especially, it seems that many are looking for something or someone outside of ourselves to *make* us happy. This is the mechanism behind our Pursuit Obsession. We keep looking for a reason, a justification, or an outside cause. However, an experience that "brings you joy" goes much deeper. It brings you to a place *within yourself* that is the *source* of your joy. It comes from an *inside* source. Experiencing joy doesn't require a reason, an outside source, or a justification. It is a state of being that has an internal point of reference.

Third, pampering nurtures your spirit and increases your inner peace. The word *nurture* means "to nourish, develop, cultivate." *Inner peace* is an "internal state of serenity, harmonious thoughts, and feeling." So as you move through this book, remember to keep bringing yourself back to this threefold definition of pampering. I suggest that you mark the previous page or fold down the upper corner so that you can refer to it easily.

After sharing my threefold criteria for pampering in my pampering seminars and workshops, I often ask participants to share personal examples of what they do to pamper themselves. In one seminar I posed this question to the group: "What brings you joy?" Barbara said that reading her sons' report cards brought her joy since they both made good grades. In another seminar Debbie said that taking her daughters to the library and checking out a book to do some personal reading while she was there brought her joy.

Upon closer examination of these two responses, you see that neither fulfills all aspects of the threefold pampering criteria. In Barbara's example she explained that she enjoyed receiving her sons' report cards because they were good students and earned good grades. And seeing their good grades made her feel proud. She was not the primary beneficiary, however. Instead she was indirectly receiving benefit, by way of her sons. I asked her to consider this question to help her get clear about the distinctions of personal pampering: Would receiving your sons' report cards still bring you joy if they earned F's instead of A's? Her answer was an immediate "Of course not!" She soon realized that her example was conditional and based on an external cause.

Now let's take a look at Debbie's example. Was she the primary beneficiary? Did the experience bring her joy, or was she simply trying to make the most of a situation? She was able to see how her example fell short of the threefold definition as well. When she did identify something that met all three criteria, this is what she came up with: composing music, writing lyrics, singing, and playing her piano. For Barbara, taking walks at sunset and reading thriller novels successfully "qualified" as pampering.

My point is this: *If you aren't in touch with what brings you joy and rejuvenates your spirit, then there is little hope for being able to incorporate more of these experiences into your life.*

We are spirit-filled beings, but the effect of being conditioned and programmed by a Euro-American Western culture leaves us lopsided and out of whack—materially overdeveloped and spiritually underdeveloped. American culture overemphasizes the material and virtually ignores the spirit. We're conditioned to focus on our physical and material needs almost to the complete exclusion of our spiritual needs.

Collectively the American culture is suffering from spiritual bankruptcy. Many of us have a spiritual void inside of us—an inner spiritual well that is dry and seeks to be filled, even if for a moment. I continue to be amazed at the lengths to which we'll go to try to fill this void, the lengths we'll go to cover up or disguise our emptiness. Then when the cover-up doesn't work, we resort to trying to drown, suffocate, and stifle this deep inner need for spiritual nourishment. Some of us will settle for a brief hit, or go for a temporary high or quick fix—even if it harms or endangers ourselves or others.

There are many ways we attempt to fill this void or numb the pain of the longing. We grasp desperately at illusions of fulfillment or what only gives us temporary satisfaction, such as having an affair, taking drugs, overeating, lying to look good, manipulating others, getting drunk, gossiping, judging others, physically abusing someone else or oneself, talking down to others, making others wrong, engaging in sexual promiscuity, power tripping, and attention-getting behaviors such as cursing others out.

After leading pampering seminars and workshops for hundreds of women around the country, I've had the opportunity to make some interesting observations about the appearance and "presence" of women who do *not* regularly pamper themselves. There are some very distinct indicators, and as I started to become keenly aware of them, I was surprised to discover how obviously it showed. In these instances a woman was showing signs of Pampering Neglect.

Below is a self-test of twenty-five indicators to help you identify possible signs of Pampering Neglect that may be showing up in your life. This self-test will assist you in assessing your level of need for consistent pampering in your life. Check off the indicators that *fully* or *partially* apply to you.

___ Unfocused
___ Unfulfilled
___ Easily angered
___ Frequently upset
___ Disorganized
___ Frequently overwhelmed
___ Frequently angry or
    pissed off
___ Very judgmental
___ Constantly restless
___ Constantly rushing
___ A chronic blamer
___ Frequently late

___ Bad complexion
___ Loss of passion
___ Overweight (too much
    weight for your bone struc-
    ture and body frame)
___ Constantly defensive
___ Very reactive
___ Chronic procrastinator
___ Jealous of other women, whom
    you perceive as "having it all"
___ Lack of depth and intimacy
    in friendships and
    relationships

___ A poor listener
✓ Prone to gossiping
✓ Have patterns of self-
   sabotage
___ A constant complainer

___ Always on the go
___ Minor bodily aches and
   pains
___ Life has become mundane
   and routine

Total up the number of items you've checked, and write your
score here: _____. Write today's date here: _____.
I've asked you to write down today's date so that you can revisit
this list in a month or two to see how your score has changed.

Interpreting Your Score

If you checked . . .

1–3 items	Your life probably reflects a high level of consistent pampering.
4–7 items	You probably pamper yourself periodically, but not consistently enough.
8–11 items	You probably pamper yourself every once in a while. There is no regularity.
12 or more items	Pampering is almost totally absent from your life. Your health is most likely being threatened.

In my seminars, these indicators of Pampering Neglect emerged as
distinct patterns among those who lacked continuous pampering in
their lives. And sure enough, the indicators were always consistent
with the personal testimonies.

At the same time I also noticed a distinct pattern among women who do regularly pamper themselves. And it went beyond their clothes, hair, nails, makeup, appearance, or weight, to a *total impression*—to their *Total Presence*. Women who regularly pampered themselves shared the common trait of being *in balance*. I noticed these women had a pattern of indicators, too, but in this case theirs were those of Being Regularly Pampered. These women's lives were organized around a philosophy of self-care as a top priority.

Check off the indicators of Being Regularly Pampered that *fully* or *partially* apply to you.

— Relaxed

— Magnetic, radiant

— Comfortable touching others

— At ease with yourself

— Good posture

— Decisive

— Willing to self-reflect

— Well groomed

— Laugh frequently and easily

— Compliment others easily

— Slow to get angry

— Smile easily

— An outer glow that others notice

— At ease in your body

— Accept compliments graciously

— Treated with respect by others

— Good listener

— Move with grace

— Spiritually grounded

— Good communicator

— Stay calm in stressful situations

Were you able to check off at least 15 of the 21 indicators? If not, that's okay. Being able to check off 15 or more can be a personal goal to strive for.

I think one of the reasons that pampering has such far-reaching effects in our lives is that it fills a spiritual void. Pampering is an act of self-love, so in the process of pampering yourself, you nourish and fortify your spirit. The most exciting news about pampering is that it creates real, tangible results in your life. This book contains the prescriptions and treatments for transformation so that you, too, can experience powerful results. The following list summarizes some of the personal results I've experienced as well as those experienced by participants from my pampering workshops and seminars. Remember, you, too, can expect these types of results over time.

Weight release
Less drama and crisis
More relaxed
Improved listening skills
More real and authentic
Laugh more
Rediscover hobbies and
    interests that have been "in
    remission"
Attract more positive,
    supportive sisterfriends
Pray more
Calmer
Improvement in outer
    appearance
Insights into your personal
    purpose
More clarity on personal goals
    and life mission

On time more
Improved interpersonal
    communications skills
Read more
Deepen existing friendships
Greater intimacy in love
    relationships
More joy out of the simple
    things in life
Less rushing
Meditate more
Eat less meat
More forgiving
Increased entrepreneurial
    urges
Desire to start exercise
    program
Desire to make a career move
Clearer complexion

Sacred Pampering Principles offers you a holistic self-care program designed to (a) address the deep-seated unconscious beliefs that drive unhealthy, self-negating decisions, choices, attitudes, actions, and behaviors about self-care; and (b) to support you in living a life that demonstrates more balance, self-love, and self-care.

2

GIVING YOURSELF THE BEST THAT YOU'VE GOT

HOW TO GET THE MOST OUT OF THIS BOOK

You are your lifetime's greatest project, a magnificent W.I.P., a Work-in-Progress and a Woman-in-Process. You are God's one-of-a-kind in all the world—a divine original. I believe that our assignment here on Earth in this lifetime is to keep evolving and refining ourselves. I believe, as human beings, we are designed for constant learning, growing, and love.

To aid us in this journey called Life, we are given the powerful gift of consciousness—our own ability to self-reflect and be aware of the Self and of our own thoughts. God knew exactly what She was doing when She created us. We are actually able to observe our thoughts! Because of this marvelous gift of consciousness we have the ability to self-reflect, to look back upon our own past actions, decisions, and behaviors and decide upon a different future action, decision, or behavior if we so choose. And the gift of free will gives us the creative ability of true choice, moment to moment, minute to minute, and day to day.

Self-reflection and freedom of choice are two important ingredients for transformation. These gifts are what enable this book to be a tool for personal transformation. For this book to be most useful, you may have to give up some things, especially if they are keeping you stuck or are not serving you. It will also require that you think, act, and *do* your life differently. We are going to go deep below the surface of your life as well as behind the scenes to examine the deep-seated thoughts and beliefs that are behind how you currently *do* your life.

CONSTRUCTIVE COACHING

Let me offer you a little coaching on how to get the most out of this book. First I suggest that you keep a pen or pencil on hand while you read so that you actually *do* the exercises. Don't just read through the exercises. Do them. Each one is purposefully designed to give you greater insight into yourself and propel you forward in your journey. Second, I suggest that you write *in* this book so that all your notes and thoughts are conveniently in one place. Third, I suggest that you underline or highlight words, phrases, or sentences that grab you. It will help them sink into your subconscious mind. Fourth, when a question is posed, please stop and actually answer it. So the overriding message of my coaching is this: Be willing to roll up your sleeves and do the work. No deposit, no return. No input, no output. No effort, no results.

You can't have a joy-filled life unless you have joy-filled minutes, hours, and days. **Intentionally creating more joy-filled moments in life is the essential purpose of pampering.** When you are "injoying," you are, *in that moment,* **be-ing** instead of **do-ing.** And you are in a state of bliss instead of dissatisfaction or depression. Most of us are *doing* life—we're doing what pays the bills. Doing what we *have* to do, are expected to do, or are told to do. And we're not experiencing enough joy.

We are pleasure-deserving, creative, joy-seeking beings at heart. If our daily lives contained more experiences of joy, we'd complain less and enjoy more, and be more preoccupied with staying committed to living instead of trying to avoid it, escape it, or numb ourselves to it. The way to be *present* to life is to fill it with joy and pleasure.

Joy feeds our souls, nourishes our spirits, and puts us in contact with the love and essence of our Creator. It makes life juicy. If we're not experiencing joy daily and weekly, we're just existing and surviving—not thriving. The moments when and where we experience joy, we are actually communing with the Creator. We experience Oneness, at-one-ment, and bliss.

The words of a West African song played for young male initiates upon the successful completion of their six-week rite-of-passage initiation captures the miracle of discovering that each of us is the door, the room, *and* the key to our own joy and happiness. There's nowhere to look but within.

So I went and knocked at the doors locked in front of me.
I craved to enter.
Oh, little did I know the doors did not lead outside.
It was all in me.
I was the room and the door.
It was all in me.
I just had to remember.

Getting clear about what brings you joy is a self-discovery process that is a critical step toward integrated self-care. Pampering yourself is about creating more meaningful moments in your life and a deeper relationship with yourself.

WHAT BRINGS YOU JOY?

The following exercise is designed to help you do just that—get in touch with what brings you joy. This exercise is a *starting* place. It includes reflecting upon your childhood. This is useful because many of us have abandoned the fun experiences, hobbies, and play we enjoyed as little girls. Our childhood represented a stage in our lives where we were freer, less inhibited, more spontaneous. But now we have sophisticated adult excuses for why our lives don't contain more joy-full activities, "reasons" such as "I've gotten too old for that" or "I don't have the time." Part of pampering's self-revelation process is getting in touch with what nourishes *your* mind, body, and spirit.

Ask yourself this question: *What brings me joy?* Give yourself at least five minutes to sit and reflect, and *then* begin writing out your list of what brings you joy. Include activities and experiences from your childhood in the right-hand column. Remember the distinctions between bringing you joy and making you happy discussed on page 14. Feel free to write in your book so that you can reference it later and continue adding to your personal Joy List.

Now, look back over your list. What are some of the things you notice about what you've written down? Any patterns? Any particu-

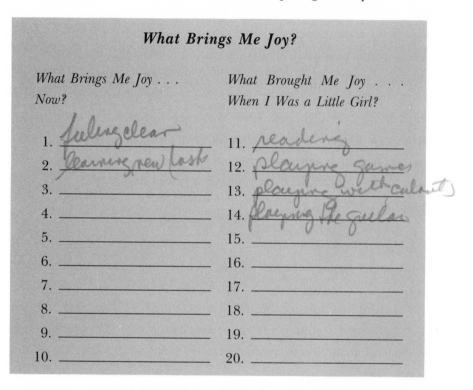

What Brings Me Joy?

What Brings Me Joy . . . Now?

1. *feeling clear*
2. *learning new task*
3. _____
4. _____
5. _____
6. _____
7. _____
8. _____
9. _____
10. _____

What Brought Me Joy . . . When I Was a Little Girl?

11. *reading*
12. *playing games*
13. *playing with color*
14. *playing the guitar*
15. _____
16. _____
17. _____
18. _____
19. _____
20. _____

lar qualities that emerge? What does your list say about you? When I have participants do this exercise in my workshops, they are usually surprised at the types of things they write down. Most of them have never asked themselves this simple but profound question. Participants' responses usually consist of inexpensive, simple things that require their energy and attention but little or no money. So experiencing them as a reality in life doesn't have to be dependent on money. In this culture we are so used to the excuses of "I don't have the money" or "It costs too much." We use these excuses as a crutch. But when we are faced with activities and experiences that cost little or no money yet have the potential for transforming our lives, we have to ask ourselves a very serious question: *So why am I not incorporating more joy-giving activities and experiences into my life?*

Keep adding to your list and revising it every two months. Keep expanding it. When I first wrote out my list, it included experiences from my girlhood such as rollerskating down the big hill in front of my house, having sleepovers, and playing tea party with my sister. Now I've started incorporating these experiences back into my adult life.

I used to live my life in a nonstop on-the-go mode. I would rush to get ready for work in the morning and then have to battle traffic to get there. At work there were projects to complete. Proposal deadlines to meet. Appointments to keep. Too many phone calls to return. And too many meetings to attend. Then after work it was off to another engagement or event several nights of the week. Weekends were no less hectic. Laundry. Housecleaning. Bills. Groceries. Errands. Places to go and people to see. It was crazy! Now that I have a husband, two little girls, a household, a training and consulting firm to run and a speaking and writing career to manage, my life is even fuller. Pampering may have been optional once, but now it is *mandatory.*

As a result of integrating pampering into my lifestyle, my life has transformed. Positive change has been experienced in *all* areas of my life. I've been able gradually to "release" forty pounds of weight; my complexion has improved; I have deeper, more intimate friendships; my appearance has changed for the better (I cut my hair into a shorter low-maintenance style and I dress in brighter, bolder colors); I eat more healthily (less pork and red meat and more water); I get more rest; I'm more creative (I've started writing poetry again and making homemade cards and gifts); I'm more patient with others; I'm more spiritually grounded (I pray and meditate regularly); I've gotten more in touch with my talents, gifts, and skills and have translated them into my training and consulting business; I focus on managing my energy, not my time; I'm more effective; I'm not as defensive; and I'm a better listener, *to name a few*. All as a result of making pampering a priority in my life.

It's never too late to reprioritize your life. It's never too late to start moving away from what isn't working and toward what is. A compelling advertisement I recently saw in *Essence* magazine reminded me of the urgency for forward motion and positive change; it reminded me that I am here but for the moment and that all I have is the here and now. Pampering is what makes here and now joyous and meaningful. So let's shift gears. Let's start to move into that new place, right now, that empowers us to begin again to create new beliefs, new attitudes, new thoughts, and new ways of being. *Sacred Pampering Principles* is your road map for the journey. But be sure to go at your own pace. *Remember, baby steps will get you there the same as big strides, it just takes a little longer.*

New Beginnings

There is a powerful rule that has been playing out in our lives with 100 percent effectiveness. I call it the One Hundred Percent Success Rule. Willis Kinnear, in his book, *Thirty-Day Mental Diet*, describes it: "For the most part, people feel that they are a success in an endeavor when it has a favorable outcome, and a failure when it is not accomplished. Closer consideration will show that *success is the achievement of the dominant idea you have in mind, and what you achieve always corresponds to your thinking* [italics, mine]." In other words we are each achieving results *all* of the time. But if our experiences are negative or undesirable, then it's time to start succeeding in something different, something more positive and empowering.

Now is the time to take a good look at your life from an objective point of view. If an observer were to shadow you for a week, what message would your behaviors and choices be sending? Your behaviors and choices are pieces of you. *They are a demonstration of your beliefs and dominant thoughts.* So what kind of style of life would emerge? Take a look at an uncensored, unedited version of your life over the course of an entire week. Be ruthlessly honest with yourself. What do the results and outcomes of your life demonstrate that you're succeeding at *right now*? Do your current results and outcomes demonstrate a love and respect of self that say:

- I value my rest, quiet time, and solitiude.
- Pampering and self-care are integrated components of my life.
- I treat my body as a temple.
- I honor my intuition.
- I love myself.
- I expend my energy on what brings me joy and pleasure.
- My personal mental, emotional, physical, and spiritual needs are a priority.
- My life actively demonstrates that I understand that pampering and self-care are not selfish but loving self-service.
- I move through my day-to-day activities with ease, grace, and peace of mind.

If your life isn't saying *these* types of things, then what *is* it saying?

From the perspective of an observer, are you putting your personal self-care needs at the bottom of your Priority Pole, constantly forgoing your own needs so that others' needs can roll along smoothly at your expense? Would this observer see you not getting quite enough rest? Never quite having enough time? Never quite allowing yourself to receive or be contributed to? What patterns, attitudes, and unhealthy behaviors do you notice?

Instead of obsessing over never having enough time, a self-caring lifestyle requires that we focus on how we use our energy. Yes, our *energy,* not our *time.* This perspective requires us to shift our attention to our energy and where, how, and with whom we *use* it. A healthier hierarchy of priorities is achieved by continuously assessing how we are spending our energy. When you shift from a time-management focus to an energy-management focus, you are shifting to a focus on *quality versus quantity.*

Taking an honest look at where, how, and with whom you use your energy now will give you insight into your *current* priorities. Where does fulfillment of *your* needs fit it? Who's ahead of you on your Priority Pole? Is it the job, kids, husband, boyfriend, lover, church, girlfriends? Where do *you* fit in?

Reflect for a moment on your priorities. Write down your priorities *as currently demonstrated by the amount of energy you devote to each,* with the first one being your top priority according to amount of energy spent.

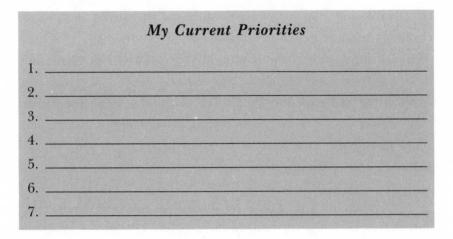

My Current Priorities

1. _____

2. _____

3. _____

4. _____

5. _____

6. _____

7. _____

How, where, and with whom do you currently spend your energy? Are you investing in people and experiences that are rewarding, satisfying, and gratifying to you? Do you need to start using your energy differently, directing it to people and experiences that bring you more joy? For many of us our current priority list reveals that we spend disproportionate amounts of energy with people and doing things that aren't really meaningful to us. Do you need to make wiser choices based upon reciprocity and positive contribution to your mental, emotional, physical, and spiritual well-being? Revisit this list periodically to assess whether use of your energy is aligned with what brings you joy and peace of mind.

Our priorities and what we consider to be important to us show up as a direct function of where, with whom, and on what we use our energy. For many of us the where, the whom, and the what are frequently not aligned with joy, pleasure, or what contributes to our growth. Instead we continue to hang out with and hang on to those that sap our energy instead of contributing to it. We spend our money on items of conspicuous consumption—acquiring, paying for, paying off, repairing, and replacing material things. But we've got to stop the insanity and ask ourselves some important questions: *What are these* things *really doing for my spirit? Is what I'm doing bringing me deep fulfillment in my life? Is the quality of my life being enhanced?*

BUSTING THE MYTHS

The word *myth* has a couple of meanings. So that you are clear about which one it is that applies to busting pampering myths, let me define it for you. I *don't* mean myths as in legends and oral traditions that are an important part of cultural continuity. Instead I'm referring to the other meaning of myth, as a fictitious idea or false notion that limits and inhibits you. To help you start dismantling some of the myths you may have around the issue of pampering, I've created the following Busting-the-Myths Exercise.

When I first did this exercise, several personal myths surfaced. Some of my myths included the following: (a) If I put self-care as a priority in my life, someone else will be left out or something will go undone; (b) self-care first is selfish and self-centered; (c) my plate is already full, and I don't have time for anything else right now; (d) yeah, pampering is nice, but it doesn't make a *real* difference; and (e) pampering is a luxury, not a necessity.

So the next step in the shift to a self-caring lifestyle is *recognizing* where you are right now. Being aware of what you're doing that's not serving you and what you're doing that is. It's a lot easier to get where you're going if you know where you're starting from. So it would be useful for you to take a look at the myths you've absorbed about pampering.

Imagine that your deep-seated thoughts and beliefs are like the celluloid film that runs through a movie projector. Your life is the projections and images that show up on the movie screen. These thoughts and beliefs have become so much a part of our mental, emotional, and psychic fabric that they've become indistinguishable to us. They've been behind the scenes, running the show. They manifest very clearly, however, in our relationships, decisions, actions, and behaviors. If we know how to change the film—which represents these underlying thoughts and beliefs—we can reconnect with our inner power to create personal change and renew ourselves. When we start to recognize and change these deep-seated thoughts and beliefs, we access the ability to positively change what shows up on the screen. Change your thoughts and beliefs and you can change your life. Creating *new* personal beliefs yields a healthier, more balanced you.

What are the deep-seated beliefs, opinions, values, and thoughts that you currently have about pampering yourself? How much importance does pampering have in your life right now? These are important questions to contemplate, because we accept our thoughts and beliefs as truth. And it is these personal truths, whether acknowledged or not, that drive our lives.

When I thought of pampering a few years ago, I had images of glamorous white women with perfect nails, perfect hair, perfect makeup, perfect bodies, and rich husbands running through my mind—women who didn't have to work and had the luxury of pampering themselves. No wonder I wasn't pampering myself! I didn't fit my *own* images! I had subconsciously adopted negative beliefs about pampering, and it was these very beliefs that were keeping me from pampering myself.

Reflect on the thoughts, beliefs, and images you have about pampering. Use the spaces below to write down your responses.

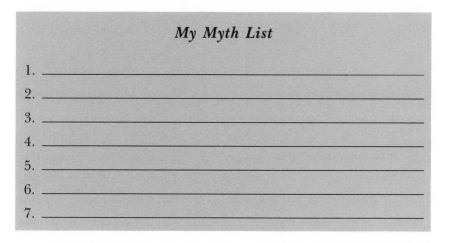

My Myth List

1. _____
2. _____
3. _____
4. _____
5. _____
6. _____
7. _____

Myths can be very damaging because they can undermine good pampering intentions. To free yourself up to treat yourself better, these myths need to be dismantled. A few years ago pampering wasn't even a consideration because my personal myths had me trapped and I didn't even know it. I knew something was missing, but I didn't know what. I simply thought I just wasn't into pampering. All the while it was my negative deep-seated thoughts, beliefs, and images I had absorbed, or received through conditioning, that kept me from considering pampering as a vital, integral ingredient of "full-filled" living. I, too, had to do the core myth-busting work.

I had to throw out my limited, programmed thinking and replace it with new beliefs, thoughts, and images that reframed pampering in a more empowering context. Take a look back at your Myth List. Reread each one and then let it know that it is *dismissed*! Strike through each as you read it. It is not serving you. It is time to release it and let it go.

PAMPERING GREMLINS

Ever notice how good we are at using convincing reasons, justifications, and circumstances to explain why we aren't taking better care of ourselves? I call excuses our Pampering Gremlins. You look up and realize that you haven't been honoring your pampering time. The reasons and excuses for why you haven't been pampering yourself regularly are your Pampering Gremlins (PGs). Our PGs can be very slick. They'll sneak in and undermine your self-care efforts if you're not careful. Notice the form and shape of the reasons, excuses, and justifications you use for not regularly pampering yourself.

For me a good excuse I was tempted to use, with a husband, two little kids, a household, a writing and speaking career, and a training and consulting firm to manage is "I don't have the time." Your PGs will try to convince you that *they* are more important than your self-care needs. They'll keep you from recognizing that loving care of self *first and foremost* empowers you to *better* take care of the other people and responsibilities in your life. The PGs I've heard women discuss in my seminars are diverse. Participants' PGs have ranged from "I work two jobs and I don't have any spare time," "I have a young baby who demands all my time," and "I don't have anyone to watch my kids," to "I don't have a reliable car." *What are your Pampering Gremlins?* Stop and ponder for a few minutes. . . . Again, this is a time to be ruthlessly honest with yourself. The more in touch you are with the types of reasons and excuses you might use for *not* regularly pampering yourself, the better you'll be at catching yourself and preventing self-sabotage later. What do you notice about your PGs? Are there any patterns or themes? The circumstance, people, or situations that tend to show up on your PGs list will reveal vulnerabilities and "soft spots" that you should be aware of. The responses that show up on your PGs list are also those that have the greatest potential for sabotaging you in your self-care efforts. So heads up!

STICKS AND STONES

Remember the old sticks-and-stones rhyme about getting your feelings hurt by someone else's words? "Sticks and stones may break my bones, but words will never hurt me!" Actually words do hurt. Spoken words can't be seen, but they are felt. Words can do damage, and the pain can last a lot longer than a punch or a kick. To the degree that words can do negative damage, they can also be used to empower you. We want to access and use positive word power as we begin making the transition to a self-caring lifestyle.

The Bible, one of our great wisdom texts, speaks of the power of words. Proverbs 18:4 says, "The words of a man's mouth are as deep waters," and Proverbs 18:7–8 says, "A fool's mouth is his destruction. . . . The words of a talebearer are as wounds, and they go down into the innermost part of the belly." In other words the tongue and the words it creates can be a dangerous weapon if misused. Words are our vehicles for relating and describing our reality. So they shouldn't be abused. Words can create a new reality. And a proverb from *The Husia,* an ancient Egyptian wisdom text, says, "The tongue of a man is his sword." So we must be mindful of the power of our words.

In Chapter 1 of Genesis it says, "In the beginning God created the heaven and the earth, and the earth was without form and void; and darkness was upon the face of the deep. . . . And God said Let there be light; and there was light." The Earth was *called forth* into being by the Word. A connection is made through sound. The language we use and the words we choose play an important part in the transformation process.

Language consists of words and symbols that have meanings, and meanings are what shape our perceptions. And our perceptions shape our reality. So when you start changing your language, you start changing meanings. When you can change meanings, you can change your reality. If you can change your reality, you can change your life. *When you start using new words, you start creating space for new meanings and new realities to emerge and come forth in your life.*

Our words are not only vehicles of communication, they also reveal our state of mind. The One Hundred Percent Success Rule reminds us that the results and outcomes we experience always correspond to our thinking. And in turn, our words become an expression of our thoughts and attitudes. They literally shape and create our reality once they are spoken. When you speak something, you give it life. We *must* pay closer attention to what comes forth out of our mouths. Words are purposeful sounds that carry meaning. Each sound has a different vibration, a different energy associated with it. So words can serve as a bridge between the visible and the nonvisible realms.

AFFIRMATIONS—POSITIVE WORD POWER

A powerful tool that paves the way for positive life change is affirmations. *To affirm* means to "make firm" or to "declare positively." An affirmation is a special kind of statement that holds within it tremendous potential for birthing change. As we make our way along this journey to joy-filled living, affirmations are like the stepping-stones. Affirmations are powerful tools for redefining who we really are and what is possible for us. So we want to understand how to tap into this positive word power and put it to full use.

Here are five guidelines for creating affirmations I've developed to help you fully tap into this positive word power. Often it is not as easy as it may seem. It takes awareness and practice to develop powerful personal affirmations. Affirmations are especially powerful tools for initiating change in particularly challenging areas of our lives. Affirmations are powerful because they allow us to state a new reality, separate and distinct from the one we may be presently experiencing. Effective affirmations have the following qualities:

- They are stated in the present tense—no past tense, no future tense, or -ed ending.
- They are personal. Use the pronoun *I* and refer to change, results, or outcomes in *yourself* rather than in someone else or in the external world.
- They are stated in the positive— avoid not, or won't or don't statements.
- They are specific, clear, and direct.
- They are to be repeated—say them frequently. Loosening up old thinking can take time.

Write your affirmations out and put them in visible places likes your daily planner, your calendar, your Bible, on your bathroom mirror, in your purse, or on the refrigerator so that you will read and reread them.

Following these guidelines may seem like a simple task at first, but it can become challenging when you try creating specific affirmations for areas of your life where you've been experiencing stagnation or frustration.

For many years, I had a weight challenge. (Notice that I said weight *challenge* and not weight *problem? New language.*) My weight was an issue from my senior year of high school up until just a few years ago. It seemed that losing weight was always on my mind. My weight seemed to be the primary focus of my attention. I always seemed to be thinking about how much I weighed. Had I gained a few pounds? Had I lost a few? What I should and shouldn't eat. What clothes I could and couldn't wear.

A few years ago I decided to commit myself to being free of this challenge. The first place I started was with positive word power—changing my language and word choices. One day when I was sitting in on one of my sisterfriend Jewel Diamond Taylor's motivational seminars, she shared how she no longer used the term *weight loss*. She explained that she had changed her language to *weight release*. She went on to explain, "Things that you lose you usually want to find, and I'm not interested in finding any weight I've lost! I want to release it—permanently!" A light clicked on inside of me when she shared this example. In that instant I began to realize how new possibilities for positive change could be initiated by *using new language*. Thus began my language change around the issue of my weight challenge.

As I pondered my weight issue further, I realized there were several other words I was also going to need to change if I was truly going to change my frame of mind. Next I addressed the word *exercise*. This word certainly didn't work for me. When I thought of the word *exercise,* it brought vivid images of breathless, funky, sweaty bodies to mind, which for me translated into sore muscles and my hair kinkin' up. And my hair kinkin' up meant a trip to the hairdresser to get my hair done. And *that* meant time and money.

So instead of continuing to resist exercising, I definitely had to replace the word *exercise* with a word that had more positive connotations and associations. So it was out with the word *exercise* and in with the word *movement.* To me the thought of *moving* more versus exercising more was appealing. I could handle increasing my amount of movement. In my mind the word *movement* was gentler. I could embrace the concept of movement because it didn't sound so intense. I set goals to move a little more here and a little more there, taking self-paced baby steps as I made positive steps toward integrating more movement into my Lifestyle.

I started parking at the not-so-convenient parking spots when I went to the store and walked the extra distance. If I had an appointment on the second or third floor of a building, I'd take the stairs instead of the elevator. While I brushed my teeth in the morning, I started doing leg lifts and lunges. I started doing a few sit-ups at night before getting into bed. And I started walking to the mailbox instead of checking the mail when I drove by on my way to an appointment.

The next word was *diet*. Diet made me think of restriction, calorie counting, a growling stomach, and of all the things I *couldn't* eat. Not very positive, empowering associations. So out with the word *diet* and in with the phrase *conscious eating choices*. These simple language changes around the issue of my weight gave me new freedom. These language changes helped me to start reframing and reshaping my mind-sets about weight. This new language triggered positive associations and activated new attitudes that were the beginning of my gradual and permanent weight release. Language changes and new word choices allow you to give new meaning to an old or familiar subject.

At the most basic level positive power helped me shift my relationship to my body and my weight. Affirmations do not sugarcoat your current situation. Instead they are tools for creating a new reality in the present tense. Going back to the five guidelines I established earlier, I'll contrast my old language with the affirmations I created to empower me in my weight-release process.

Old Language	*Affirmations (New Language)*
INSTEAD OF . . .	REPLACE WITH . . .
• I want to lose weight.	• I release weight easily and effortlessly.
• I should be exercising regularly.	• I enjoy my daily movement activity.
• I'm on a diet.	• I make conscious eating choices that serve me and support my body temple.

Now you give it a try. Pick a specific area related to self-care where you are experiencing a challenge or frustration. Then work on creating a present-tense, positive, personal, specific affirmation to support you in replacing negative thoughts and beliefs with affirming ones. Here are a few to help you get started:

I am worthy of being pampered.

I understand the importance of regularly pampering myself.

Pampering and self-care increase my appreciation and love of self.

Pampering and self-care empower me to care better for others.

I make room for regular self-pampering in my life.

My body is a divine creation worthy of tender, loving care and attention.

Pay attention to the language you and others use around the issue of pampering. The most magnificent thing about affirmations is that they really work. But remember, they must be repeated and practiced diligently. Replacing old language with new language requires attention, time, practice, and discipline. Affirmations work because they unlock the gates of change within you. They create a new internal state of mind, which in turn initiates change in your outer state of affairs.

3

SACRED PAMPERING
PRINCIPLES FOR THE SPIRIT

I define the *soul* as the center of your Essence, the core of your unique being, and the *spirit* as the vital life-giving Godforce that infuses and fills your physical body. Our focus in the Euro-American Western culture is on the needs of the physical body to the exclusion and detriment of the spirit. We are taught how to wash our faces, brush our teeth, comb our hair, and put on our clothes, but the spiritual self has been largely neglected out of ignorance. If we had been taught, as little girls, how to pamper ourselves regularly, I don't think we'd have such a hard time with it as grown women. Nurturing our spirits would be considered a standard ingredient of our personal upkeep.

At the heart of pampering are the following 24 sacred pampering principles, 12 for the spirit and 12 for the body. As you embark upon this journey, remember that the word *sacred* means "highly valued" and "worthy of respect." And a *principle* is "a highly honored fundamental." Buckle up and enjoy yourself!

SACRED PAMPERING PRINCIPLE FOR THE SPIRIT #1—
FALLING IN LOVE WITH YOU

Many of us are, as the song goes, "looking for love in all the wrong places." We're looking to others, we're looking high and low, and we are trying desperately to be in the right place at the right time. In my seminars and workshops on healthy love relationships I continuously encounter women who are frustrated, angry, and disappointed. They are disappointed because they've been searching for love *outside* themselves, and the search has been futile—it has left them disillusioned, lonely, and often bitter. When we go about looking for love outside ourselves, we project unattainable expectations onto others. We hope that someone else will fill the place within us that can only be filled *from within*. If you think it happens any other way, you've bought into a false illusion. Love is not *found*. *You tap into the love within and allow it to express through you.*

We keep hopin' and believin' that once we get into the "right" relationship or find the "right" man, everything will be all right. This belief is a setup for disappointment. And it is also why many of us go through life with empty "containers" of self-love, hoping to get it filled by others—whether it's through church, our jobs, our children, or food, sex, or drugs. In order to have our containers of self-love filled, it requires that we thoroughly understand our Source. We've got to get *in tune* with our Source. And this Source is God/Goddess, the Creator working through you. When you get in tune with yourself, you also get in tune with your Source, the Creator. The Source works in and through each one of us. The key to being fulfilled is tapping into your Source purposefully and ongoingly.

You experience being full-filled when you tap into the Source and *allow* love to flow in you and through you to others. Allowing self-love requires self-acceptance. This means loving yourself *just* the way you are, *in spite of* your flaws, imperfections, rough edges, and past mistakes. Loving yourself is like building a house upon a rock-solid foundation. Self-love is the foundation. It determines our staying power and is what enables the house to weather the storms and the seasons of change.

Once when I was leading a love-relationships workshop, I stopped to ask the group of women, "What kind of things would you do if you were in love with the most wonderful person in the world?" After a few seconds of silence while they contemplated the question, women started to raise their hands to respond. As I went around the room calling on women, they shouted out all kinds of delicious and exciting possibilities including candlelight dinners, reading poetry, massages, long Sunday-afternoon drives, walks on the beach, and love letters. At the end of this outpouring of re-sponses I told them that the most wonderful person in the world was sitting in their own seats. I told them that they would be looking her in the face if they were to look in the mirror. They were speech-less. Mouths dropped open. They all had assumed I was talking about someone *other* than themselves—a wonderful *man*. Mr. Right, no doubt! Then I posed this question: "Are you doing all of those wonderful things *with* and *for yourself*, right *now*? If not, *why* not? What are you waiting for? Are you waiting until Mr. Right comes along before you start actively demonstrating your love for yourself, hoping that he can fill the places in you that are in need of love?" If you're not spending quality time with you, what makes you think anyone else would want to? You have to *be* to and for yourself whatever it is you are looking for someone else to give you emotionally and spiritually. In turn, as living magnets we attract others into our lives who are whole and self-loving.

Women who love and respect themselves demonstrate it. It shows. I can easily spot a woman who is self-loving. She has a certain walk, a certain posture, a warm smile, she makes eye contact. She has a positive energy about her. She is comfortable touching and hugging others. She is not squeezed into clothes that are too tight. She has an air of ease and grace about her. She exudes a radiance and an inner glow. *Is your self-love flowing and showing?*

SACRED PAMPERING PRINCIPLE FOR THE SPIRIT #2— GETTING ACQUAINTED WITH YOU

Do you know you? I mean *really* know you? Separate from your family name, your job title, the hats you wear, your degree, your roles, and your family's definition of you? Tomorrow morning while you're getting ready for your day, after you finish brushing your teeth, pause for one full minute. For one full minute look *into* yourself in the mirror instead of *at* yourself. Lean in toward the mirror and look deep into your own eyes. What do you feel? What thoughts and emotions come up?

In the ancient Egyptian mystery schools, initiates were taught that the single most important task in life was to "Know Thyself." I believe that regardless of the circumstances of *how* we came into the world, we are each here for a divine purpose, a divine assignment. As I continue to stretch, grow, evolve, and discover more of myself, I continue to get clearer on my assignment, my divine purpose, my life mission. Part of "getting acquainted with you" is getting clear on the unique combination of gifts, talents, skills, and abilities that make *you* up, that distinguish you from the other people on this planet.

Seeking Out Your True Self

Many of us are suffering from an identity problem because we've arrived at who we consider ourselves to be via *other* people's definitions and expectations of us. Western culture has a propensity for insidiously applying pressure on us to conform while masquerading itself as an accepting, flexible, and tolerant culture. This type of environment undermines our personal power and stifles self-expression.

From the time we are little girls, we are bombarded with so many *should*s and *supposed to*s that we lose our Selves in the process. As we are socialized, we begin to construct an identity defined by our parents, our degree, our level of education, our looks, our job, our socioeconomic status, which side of the tracks we lived on, our IQ, our skin color, our weight. It can be a struggle sifting through all of this to find who you really are, *distinct* from all of this, instead of being defined *by* all of this. Fuel is added to this morass of conflicting messages when we are taught to believe that we *are* our bodies instead of spiritual beings that *have* bodies.

I was touched and deeply moved by a September 1995 Barbara Walters interview with actor Christopher Reeve, known best for his Superman roles, after he had taken a headfirst fall from a horse that paralyzed him from the neck down. For the interview he sat in his motorized wheelchair, complete with special gadgets, levers, and a neck support to help keep his head in place. When Barbara Walters asked what he had learned from this experience, his vivid blue eyes sparkled brightly, and without hesitation he smiled and replied, "I've learned that I am *not* my body."

Many of us live and die and never make that critical distinction. We invest *so* much time, energy, and money in dressing up our bodies, and overworking our bodies that we haven't taken the time to get to know the indwelling spirit. Getting acquainted with you is about going beyond your physical packaging to get in touch with your spiritual Being, your true nature, the distinct qualities that make you an individual expression of the Creator.

SACRED PAMPERING PRINCIPLE FOR THE SPIRIT #3— INNERCISE: TONING UP YOUR SPIRIT

"Innercise" is working on the Self from the inside out. At the crux of Innercise is *self-reflection* and inner growth. Taking time-outs to reflect and contemplate tones and strengthens our spirits. We each go through the necessary Innercise when we're ready, because it's a self-paced process. I believe that we attract the experiences, people, circumstances, and situations into our lives and across our paths that help us evolve, grow forward, and go forward. Innercise is the result of honest self-evaluation, especially around ego issues. Our ego issues can show up in many ways: defensiveness, anger, jealousy, gossiping, backstabbing, conceit, control issues, and dishonesty. The more your ego is running the show, the more these types of issues are present in your life. Innercise is the process of moving through these issues and seeing them as indicators of where we are in need of more love and more spiritual work in our lives. When you understand the importance of Innercise, you stop and reflect in order to seek out the messages and the growth lessons for your ego. This ability to self-reflect allows you to extract the good from every experience.

The simplified formula for Innercise is:

Pause . . . Reflect . . . Assess . . . Realize . . . Learn . . . Integrate
= Innercise

We especially have lots to learn from people and situations that piss us off or get us upset. Our typical ego response is to (a) decide that the other person/situation is the problem; (b) avoid the person/situation; or (c) write off the person/situation as being wrong. For example you have a woman in your office who really gets on your nerves. You can avoid her, ignore her, decide she has a problem, or all of the above. *Or* you can ask yourself, "What buttons in me is she able to push? Why? What areas of growth in me does this point to?" These types of questions promote Innercise and help direct us to the inner parts of ourselves that need more refining. Many of us do everything we can to avoid and deny what's real. Especially when it comes to facing the spiritual self-work and ego-work that we need to do. The very parts of us that get stirred up, activated, or triggered in these situations are the unrefined parts of our ego. Innercise begins when we stop to reflect, focus, and assess what in *us* is getting activated, pissed off, or frustrated. Then we must take personal responsibility for our reactions instead of placing and projecting blame onto an outside source. Every ego flare-up is an opportunity for insight into ourself—where the potential for real learning and growth resides.

SACRED PAMPERING PRINCIPLE FOR THE SPIRIT #4— SPIRIT-NOURISHING TOOLS

If we were preparing to build a house, there would be certain tools we'd need in order to be well equipped—a hammer, a level, and a handsaw, for example. Then we'd also need supplies. Tools are different from supplies, however. And we don't want to get the two confused. Nails, lumber, sheetrock, screws, and cement are supplies. Supplies are *consumed* in building the house, whereas tools are the aids used to assist us in *performing* the work. We are familiar with both the tools and the supplies we need when it comes to building *external* things, but how familiar are we with the tools needed for *inner building,* for nourishing our spirits? Let's take a look at the kinds of tools and experiences that enrich and renew the spirit.

If we take a look around this country, we see the glaring signs of lack of spiritual nurturing. As a whole, America, the epitome of Western culture, is a nation of spiritually starved people. This is a dangerous condition. When you aren't being spiritually nourished, you start pursuing things outside of yourself in an attempt to fill the void. Unfortunately we often don't consider the needs of our spirit until *after* we reach a near-breaking point or are almost at the end of our rope. Then all of a sudden it becomes urgent. We work our hands to the bone, or get overwhelmed and fed up. *Then,* in an effort to maintain our sanity, we go underground to save ourselves. We get sick, go into a depression, or withdraw from the world for a while. We don't want to answer the phone, talk to anyone, or even get out of bed. We just don't want to play anymore.

In a candid interview in *Essence* magazine several years ago, Oprah Winfrey shared some insights into her personal journey toward a self-caring lifestyle. There was a point in her career when she was taping two of her daily talk shows a day while also taping the TV show *Brewster Place* in the evenings. She explained that she had been running herself ragged and that she'd gotten to the point where she was mentally and physically exhausted. She was literally working around the clock and, in the process, barely keeping her sanity. She soon came to the realization that she desperately needed to slow down, to do some inner listening, to get centered, and to pamper herself.

None of us should have to push ourselves almost to our breaking point before we realize the need to connect with our inner selves and put care of self *first* in our lives. Our inner well-being powerfully and profoundly affects our mental, spiritual, and physical well-being. Can you imagine driving your car thousands of miles without taking it in for routine maintenance? What would happen to your car if you got so busy that you didn't maintain it regularly? If you didn't take it in for an oil change, tune-up, tire rotation, battery check, wheel alignment, or washing? I've discovered that the results are much the same with human beings. When we don't take regular time-outs to tune up and refuel our spirits, we break down and our "engines" lock up.

This may seem like an oversimplification, but it's true. With our car, the lack of regular maintenance erodes its life, and it shows: a squealing fan belt, squeaky brakes, worn tire treads, or a noisy muffler. In much the same way a lack of ongoing personal pampering takes a toll on us individually and collectively. And the signs and indicators of our neglect manifest in our minds, bodies, and spirits. The symptoms show up in various ways. For example, are you often behind schedule? Do you constantly procrastinate? Do you get too little sleep? Do you feel worn out at the end of your typical day? Are you constantly rushing or on the go? Do you often feel stressed out or worried? Do you find yourself harboring resentment toward others? Do you feel that you never have enough time for adequate personal grooming? Do you participate in "self-pity parties?" Do any of these signs and indicators ring true for you? If you are like most of us, at least a couple of them do.

The journey to an integrated self-caring lifestyle is an ongoing process that requires you to make full use of the spirit-nourishing tools that are available to you. The tools in your spiritual toolbox are important companions for your self-care journey. Set a goal of building up your spiritual toolbox and putting each tool to use.

Spiritual Tool #1—Breath

Breathing keeps us alive. Breath inspires us. *To Inspire* means "to fill with high emotion, stimulate to creativity, or affect by divine influence." Breath is the vital force that animates us, yet we take it for granted. Many of us aren't fully accessing our ability to feel deeply or live passionately because we aren't *breathing* deeply. Our relationship with the Creator is shallow because our breathing is shallow. We aren't fully taking in our essential life force, and thus we aren't fully taking in life. We can go without food for over thirty days, water for three to four days, but breath we can't go without for more than a *minute*. Breathing is automatic, yet critical. We act as if our next breath is guaranteed, *a given, for certain,* when actually our next breath could very well be our last.

Most of us breathe from the upper chest instead of from deep in our bellies. We inhale only into our chest cavity, and our divine life force doesn't reach in to our lower abdomen, where correct breathing should be concentrated. Our body's seven chakras, or energy centers, are only partially charged and our breathing rhythm has gotten off. And it's been off from about the age of two or three, when our socializing process really kicked in. We suck in our stomachs and fill up our chests when we inhale, and deflate the chest and stomach when we exhale. This is incorrect breathing. Correct breathing is actually the *opposite* of how we currently do it. To fully charge all seven of our body's primary energy centers, our bellies should expand outward like a balloon being blown up when we inhale, and when we exhale, our bellies should contract and relax. Correct breathing pulls the life force farther down into our bodies so that our entire being is energized and all of our chakras get "charged up."

How we breathe has a profound effect on our lives. When our lives are tight and constricted, it usually follows that our breathing is tight and constricted too. Susan L. Taylor, in her acclaimed book *Lessons in Living,* urges us to "Surrender to your breath. Surrendering to your breath is surrendering to God. . . . The stingy little breaths we live on each day sap our energy and exacerbate stress and strain." To start opening up to the flow of pleasure, joy, and creativity, you've got to start by opening up the channel—your body is this channel. To open up to the flow more fully, start with learning to breathe correctly and more deeply—in a way that brings more inspiration and vitality into your body.

As babies coming out of the womb, our very first breath is one of the deepest and fullest that we ever take. As we get older and move through our "terrible twos," we are bombarded with admonishments, warnings, and restrictions on our self-expression and actions. We are socialized and conditioned by a barrage of disempowering words and phrases, such as *no, don't, stop that, sit down, shut up,* and *get over here.* And with each additional negative admonishment our spirits get more and more suppressed. In turn our breathing gets progressively more shallow, suppressed, and constricted, to the point that we stop breathing deeply and correctly from our diaphragm and belly and convert to restricted breathing from our chest area. In other words, being socialized has the effect of shutting us down and dulling our full expression of emotion, creativity, passion, and joy. And thus the strength of our personal connection with the Creator gradually weakens.

Breathing fully and deeply accomplishes several profound objectives: (a) It allows you to feel and experience emotion more deeply and intensely; (b) it helps you stay present and in the moment instead of trying to escape; and (c) it expands your "peace core."

In *Energy Ecstasy and Your Seven Vital Chakras,* Bernard Gunther explains the connection between breathing and living fully. Breath is "a flowing bridge between life and death, every breath is rebirth, inspiration for integration, growth and re-creation. A non-with-hold, a letting go of the old." He goes on to say,

> *Change your breathing and you will think/feel differently, and this change can be created by choice, because breathing is one of the few bodily functions that can be voluntary or automatic. Depression is deep pressing against breathing. It's almost impossible to be depressed when you are breathing naturally and correctly. The problem is that most people don't breathe correctly, they only half breathe, and therefore, they are only half alive.*

Being conscious about my breathing has helped me in numerous ways. Even after speaking in front of many, many groups and to thousands of people over the years, I still get nervous a few minutes before I step up to the microphone for a speech or presentation. Now, as preparation, I take several deep "correct" breaths. This has a natural calming effect on me. It slows down my heart rate, calms my nerves, relaxes me, and helps me stay present to the moment. When I step up to the podium, I am now a much more relaxed and effective speaker.

Thanks to my breath work I am now able, *authentically and fully,* to listen without feeling compelled to get defensive when someone has a criticism of something I have done or said. It is not easy to listen to criticism without feeling compelled to explain or defend yourself. I used to be on guard and tense in these situations, as if I was waiting for a bomb to be dropped on me. My breathing would start to speed up and my breaths would get short. And I wasn't fully attentive because I was so busy devising my comeback as the person was talking.

Now I remember to breathe consciously and deeply when I am receiving constructive feedback (instead of criticism, new language) whether it's from my husband, a sisterfriend, or a family member. I've stopped resisting and fighting constructive feedback, perceiving it as a personal attack, and I've started hearing it as valuable insight for further refinement of my character. Instead of trying to justify or defend my position I listen for understanding, striving to be sure I'm fully hearing the person out.

On a spiritual and physiological level deep, conscious, correct breathing also charges all seven of your chakras, your body's energy centers. Your body's seven primary energy centers, or chakras, are located sequentially from the base of your spine up to the top of your head. Here's a summary of your seven vital chakras, starting at the top with your seventh chakra and moving down to your first:

Chakra	Description	Physical Location
Seventh	Crown Chakra	Top of the head
Sixth	Third Eye/Brow Chakra	Between the eyebrows
Fifth	Throat Chakra	Throat area
Fourth	Heart Chakra	Middle of the chest
Third	Solar Plexus Chakra	In the navel area
Second	Spleen Chakra	Just above the pubic-hair line, genital area
First	Base or Root Chakra	Parallel to the base of the spine

Correct breathing literally charges up all seven of your chakras. In *Ritual Systems of Ancient Black Civilizations,* Ra Un Nefer Amen I says that management of the breath is the key to meditation, and that the key to breath is in the management of posture. Our every-day posture resembles a letter *C,* in which our abdomen is sunken and our back is slightly hunched. This posture, which feels natural to most of us, automatically forces our breathing into our upper chest area. We are forced to breathe incorrectly, since this posture only allows for shallow breathing from the chest area. Correct pos-ture for correct breathing requires that the shoulders be straight instead of slumped or curved forward. The spine should be in a slight *S* shape instead of a *C.* Slightly lifting the chin helps you to open up your chest and abdomen area. Correct posture fosters deeper and fuller correct breathing, from the lower abdomen.

Spiritual Tool #2—Meditation

You may be asking, What exactly is meditation and how do I do it? The word *meditation* may conjure up images of a New Ager sitting on a mat with closed eyes and legs crossed in lotus position chanting "Ooooommm." Meditation is not something reserved for New Agers, yogis, or Buddhists. It is an *essential* spiritual tool that can do us all good. *To meditate* simply means "to think deeply and quietly, to ponder, to consider at length, to contemplate." Thus meditation and conscious breathing go hand-in-hand; proper man-agement of your breath can help you reach a state that is more conducive to contemplation, relaxation, and deep thought. Sitting in a chair or on the floor on a pillow are a couple of positions you might try when you meditate.

One of my favorite descriptions of meditation is provided by Margo Anand in her book *The Art of Sexual Ecstasy.* She says,

> *Imagine a bottle filled with sand and water. Shake it, and you can't distinguish a thing. This is the way the human mind functions during most of our normal, daily, waking life. It is processing so many thoughts, perceptions, and pieces of information that it is continuously "blurred." Often the circuits are jammed. But if you set the bottle down and leave it for a few minutes, the sand will arrange itself in harmonious layers on the bottom, and the water will become clear. In a way, meditation does the same.*

Even medical research, especially the inroads forged by Herbert Benson, M.D., has shown us that a meditative state actually invokes what Benson calls the relaxation response, an integrated set of physical changes that accompany the meditative state. These physiological changes include decreases in heart rate, drops in blood pressure, and improvements in immune system functioning. Scientific studies have also shown that meditation energizes and balances the left and right hemispheres of the brain, in addition to accessing "hidden" brain functions. Meditation is also reported to positively affect learning ability, behavior, and recall.

So here's a basic five-step introduction to a simple meditation style based on a technique called yoga breathing. Yoga breathing follows a breathing pattern that is opposite what we consider to be our regular "in and out" pattern, as mentioned earlier. Yet, it is our correct breathing pattern, the pattern that we followed up until we were about three years old:

1. Begin with assuming the proper **S** posture, sitting on a firm surface. Shoulders back so as to open up your lower abdomen area.
2. Close your eyes (especially recommended if you're a beginner).
3. Allow your tongue to gently rest against the roof of your mouth with the tip of your tongue on the gumline where your gums meet your teeth.
4. Inhale smoothly and slowly through your nose, *allowing your lower abdomen to inflate* as if you have a potbelly.
5. Breathe out slowly through your mouth, while allowing your lower abdomen to gently contract and deflate.

This is correct breathing. This may feel awkward at first because its a reversal of the pattern you're used to following. Continue working on this yoga breathing technique, especially when you meditate, until it becomes your new "natural" style of breathing. It took me almost a month to shift from my "normal" chest breathing to correct, lower-abdomen breathing.

Spiritual Tool #3—Prayer

One of my sisterfriends describes prayer as speaking to God, and meditation as listening. *A Course in Miracles* defines prayer as "the medium for miracles" and a "means of communications of the created with the Creator." So together prayer and meditation are powerful means of communion with the Creator. When it comes to prayer as a spirit-nourishing tool, I believe that a serious negative conditioning job has been done on our minds by traditional religion. I remember growing up in traditional Southern-style Baptist churches, in which the preacher urged us to "call on Jesus," and "lay our burdens on the Lord." This led me to believe, from a very young age, that prayer was a form of pleading, begging, and turning to God when you were in a state of desperation or helplessness. Not a very powerful perception of prayer.

Before I could move on to embrace a more empowering definition of prayer as divine communication, I first had to realize that I had absorbed limiting messages at a young age. This shift in my perception of prayer was a gradual process, but prayer has now become an active, integral part of my life. Prayer is a powerful link to the Creator because it requires that we stop, focus, and connect with our Source.

Prayer is an underutilized spiritual tool. To fully access the awesome power of prayer, we need to understand that there are different types of prayer. More important, *we need to know which type to use* given our situation, our circumstances, *and* the results we are seeking. In my personal journey I've found that understanding the distinctions of prayer has enabled me more fully to access the power of this divine communication. So let's take a closer look at some of the major different types of prayer so that it can start to play a more integral, powerful role in your life.

Prayers of Affirmation

An affirmative prayer doesn't speak to the past or present, it speaks to and calls forth a *new future* in the present. Affirmative prayers are effective because they are spoken in the *present* tense. In your mind fast-forward to your desired outcome and then speak it *as if* it is already done. For example before a presentation I visualize doing a great job and getting a great response. I visualize the details of the presentation, including my gestures, my voice inflection and volume, and the faces of the audience, showing expressions of enjoyment. I then convert this vision into an affirmative prayer, affirming these results in the present tense.

Prayers of Healing

Healing prayer works for both physical and emotional healing. I believe that dis-ease is a manifestation of unwholeness at the spiritual level. Once we release and unblock the stagnating energy that is causing the dis-ease, healing can occur. Physically I've "cleared" myself of sore throats, lower back pain, a severe neck spasm, and an impending bladder infection through the healing power of prayer combined with visualization. I use Louise Hay's book, *You Can Heal Your Life,* as a guide to help me identify the probable emotional or mental cause of the dis-ease. Then I create an inner image of healing taking place and conclude with a healing prayer that incorporates affirmations to "erase" or reprogram the thoughts and beliefs at the root cause level that are manifesting as dis-ease.

Prayers of Denial

Prayers of denial are intended to refuse to accept as truth that which is reported to be true; to refuse to accept as lasting or right anything that is not satisfying or good. I constantly deny lack and limitation in my life, and I also deny sickness, especially when I'm experiencing the early symptoms of a possible cold.

Prayers of Meditation and Silence

Prayers of meditation and silence require that you focus upon a few meaningful words and contemplate them silently. As you contemplate them, they grow in your mind as expanded ideas that move you to right action, or give you a peaceful assurance that all is well and no action is needed. Two that I frequently use are "Be still and know that I am God" and "God is love, I am Love."

Prayers of Forgiveness

Forgiveness can be instantaneous or it can be a long process. Though we've been taught to believe that forgiving someone else lets *them* off of the hook, it actually frees *us* up. Forgiveness prayer is personally liberating. It frees up both the forgiven *and* the forgiver. When you forgive, you "give for" something greater. When you forgive, you become more committed to the good than to the grudge. You release the emotional grip that a person, a situation, or a circumstance has on *you* so that you can "give for" your Higher Good. Forgiveness keeps creating vacuums in your life so that your greater good can come in. When you forgive, you release the bitterness and resentment associated with the person, situation, or circumstance.

Prayers of Thanksgiving

Prayers of thanksgiving demonstrate gratitude for experiences, lessons, insights, answers, resources, guidance, healing, provisions, or manifestations.

Prayers of Invocation

The word *invoke* means "to call on." A prayer of invocation calls on the spirit of God or the ancestors to come into a place. This prayer is often done at the beginning of a ceremony or service. At my wedding, which was done African style, we poured a libation at the beginning of the ceremony and performed a ritual to call in the ancestors. At the beginning of the Pacific Northwest African-American Women's Advance, we begin by calling in the ancestors as well. I've found that an invocation creates the sense of a more sacred, intimate environment in which those present are able to connect more deeply to the experience.

Prayers of Praise

Praise may well be considered the highest form of prayer. In a prayer of praise you are rejoicing. You become a living, breathing *demonstration* of the Creator's glory. *Hallelujah* is a common word of praise.

Prayers of Supplication

Supplication is a humble prayer of request or earnest appeal for supply of something. You are asking the Creator for certain provisions (for example courage, boldness, humility, patience, your own transportation, etc.).

Prayers of Benediction

This is a blessing usually done at the close of a ritual or worship. A benediction brings completion to the process. It brings closure and is often done at the end of a ceremony or service.

*   *   *

Taking the time to discuss the various types of prayer is not meant to make praying a cumbersome, complex activity. Instead it is meant to help you become more aware of the different forms of prayer and how to more utilize it fully as a divine communication link with the Creator.

Spiritual Tool #4—Quiet Time

Quiet Time is time set aside with no talking or distracting noises. It gives your mind and body a break. We all need breaks. I mean more than just our nightly sleep, but rather *intentional* quiet time in the form of stillness and relaxation—an intentional pause for the purpose of conscious breathing, suspending our incessant mind chatter, and giving ourselves a break from *doing*. Quiet Time, henceforth referred to as Q.T., consists of both times of silence and times for relaxation. It is Solitary Refinement.

We often don't give our Selves the same courtesy that we give the machines we use. Daily living tends to keep our muscles and bodies in a moderate to high level of tenseness, to which we have grown accustomed. Our washing machines get a break, our cars get a break, our microwave ovens get a break, even our TVs get a break. Our limiting personal myths and negative programming lead us to believe, however, that Quiet Time results in decreased productivity. To the contrary, studies have shown that those who integrate Q.T. into their weekly living routines tend to be more focused, clear thinking, effective, productive, and relaxed.

For example, I try to schedule my appointments with clients on Tuesdays, Wednesdays, and Thursdays while my daughters are at day care. Even then, when I have an intense client schedule, I try to integrate Q.T. into my day by making space for it either before or after an appointment. This allows me to take a breather, reflect, and then mentally prepare for my next appointment. Sometimes I am able to allow a one-and-a-half-hour block between appointments so that I can escape to Barnes & Noble bookstore to chill out with a soothing almond latte espresso and make some notes or write in my journal. And I try to leave Fridays open as my "play and pampering" day. As a result of integrating Q.T. into my work schedule I am able to maintain my high energy when I am with clients. Time and again they've complimented me on my ability to be consistently pleasant, positive, and energetic. This is largely a result of the mandatory Q.T. that I integrate into my daily schedule.

If you have a highly structured or rigid work schedule, your lunchtime may be your biggest span of free time. Lunchtime can be used for your Quiet Time. Here are a few suggestions on how you might use that time:

• Bring a sack lunch and stay in your office and read while you enjoy your lunch.
• Change into your tennis shoes and take a gentle stroll at lunch.
• Go to a nearby coffee shop or café by yourself and update your goals and dreams, do a crossword puzzle, or crochet or knit, whatever is relaxing to you.
• Take off your shoes, pull up a second chair, and prop up your feet for a few minutes. This helps improve the circulation in your legs and feet.
• Get a pedicure.

• Take ten-minute morning and afternoon Quiet Time breaks.
• If you belong to a health or fitness club that has a pool or Jacuzzi, take a short dip after work (which you can do without getting your hair wet) to refresh yourself before heading home.

There are other simple ways to build Quiet Time into your day before and after work. Once you get home, take ten minutes of "peace and quiet" to chill out in your bedroom, bathroom, or other quiet place before shifting into "busy gear" at home. If you have kids, let them know that you do not want to be disturbed for ten minutes. These ten minutes of chill-out time as soon as you get home is much like the decompression process deep-sea divers go through before they return to the surface. The decompression chamber helps their bodies to readjust. Consider these ten minutes of Q.T. as your decompression time. Also try Family Quiet Time. Declare one night a week the TV-Free Zone: no TV for the entire evening. I suggest that you decide together upon the chosen TV-Free night and also share the purpose for having Family Quiet Time so that it doesn't feel like "mom's new rule."

In the mornings as you get ready for work is another opportunity for Quiet Time in preparation for your workday. When you're in the bathroom, close the door, light a candle, and turn off the light. This is a great time for a meditative prayer. Either standing, or sitting on the closed toilet seat, focus on a few key phrases such as "I am at peace." Before your prayer take three deep cleansing breaths, inhaling through your nose to the count of five and exhaling through your mouth to the count of seven. These few minutes of Solitary Refinement can help you stay grounded so that you

can more gracefully cope with whatever your day has in store
for you.

After all, Q.T. isn't about doing nothing. It's about choosing
solitude as a conscious, constructive ingredient of balanced living.

Spiritual Tool #5—Journaling

Journaling is a crucial self-discovery tool. Journaling enables you
to record your thoughts, experiences, and feelings. Journaling frees
you from keeping thoughts trapped inside your head. It allows you
to capture your contemplations and insights. Writing helps put you
in touch with a deeper part of yourself. By design, journaling requires taking *time* to do it. I think the real reason more of us don't
journal is that we don't take the time, more than that we're just
"not into" journaling.

Journaling also requires getting past negative beliefs you may
have such as "I hate to write" or "I'm not a writer." We've been
taught that there is a right way to write and a wrong way to write.
When we were in school, writing was not a pleasurable experience
for most of us. It was more like pulling teeth. In school we were
forced to write essays and term papers. And the joy of it was taken
from us, along with the value and the freedom that writing as a
form of self-expression affords.

When you journal, you have permission to break the rules. You
can use pictures, symbols, cartoons, or mindmaps. Experiment with
crayons, markers, colored ink. Write while sitting in bed, lying
under a tree, or listening to music. Do what suits you. It's all okay.
Writing is a useful form of self-expression, and it can actually serve

as therapy for the soul. *A pampered woman is one who is in touch with her thoughts and feelings and is always looking for ways to gain insight into herself.* Journaling is a tool for getting to know yourself better.

Journaling gives you deeper insight into yourself, but it takes discipline. To help myself journal regularly, I've made it into a sensuous experience. I buy beautiful journals and sleek, colorful writing pens and save them especially for my journaling. I have a total of five ongoing journals, each for a different purpose—business ideas, goals and affirmations, poetry, revelations and insights, and recording my dreams.

Journaling can also be a tool for helping you through times of change and transition, challenge, or if you are in need of clarity on an issue. On one occasion I used journaling to help me move through a block I had with my weight release. I had plateaued for three months at the same weight and my weight-release process seemed to have come to a grinding halt. Though I was still eating right and doing my movement, I had stagnated and I couldn't figure out why. After losing forty pounds I was only seven pounds away from reaching my ideal weight.

In hopes of gaining some insight into this three-month-long plateau, I decided to do a spontaneous-style journaling exercise. It's a free-form style in which I don't edit or censor what I'm writing. I just let the thoughts flow from my mind and through my hand onto the paper—leaving out periods, commas, and capitals if I want to. Before I started my journaling, I posed these questions to myself: "Debrena, why are you hanging on to these final seven pounds? What are you resisting? What would it mean if you released these final seven pounds and reached your desired weight?"

As I relaxed and let my thoughts and feelings flow onto the paper, an interesting response started to unfold:

> *Releasing these final seven pounds will be my ultimate victory, and I'm afraid. Over the past few years so much of my time and energy has centered around my weight—what I should eat but didn't, what I did eat and shouldn't have, what clothes made my thighs look slimmer, which shirts and jackets were long enough to cover my hips and butt. Now here I am about to taste the success of a long-awaited victory and I'm afraid of it. Afraid of the sweetness of the victory. Afraid of the final liberation.*

My journaling helped me get in touch with my unconscious fear of success with my weight release. It helped me dig deep and confront the truth about why I had plateaued for so long. At the end of this journal entry I created some affirmations to help neutralize these disempowering thoughts and break the yoke of my fear. I wrote, "I release these final seven pounds easily and effortlessly. I deserve a fit, healthy, slim body. I love my body." This particular spontaneous journaling process was the beginning of my breakthrough.

Journaling has become a very important tool in my life. I keep journals around in convenient places—in my bedroom on my nightstand, in my office, on my altar, and one in my attaché. Since I get brainstorms at the strangest of times, I always want to be prepared to capture the thought or idea on paper. Sometimes a poem wants to come forth, sometimes it's a series of deep, provoking questions about myself, human nature, or a current event.

Sometimes I draw pictures. Sometimes I record an idea for a seminar or workshop topic. My thoughts are extremely important to me, even if they aren't to anybody else. So I see my journal as a living archive of my thoughts and ideas. The more ways I can find to express myself to myself, the better I understand, know, and love myself.

SACRED PAMPERING PRINCIPLE FOR THE SPIRIT #5— TUNING IN

Shifting from living life from an *external* point of reference to an *internal* point of reference, one that is in sync with your intuition, is what Tuning In is about. Tuning In is about sharpening up and sensitizing your ability to listen and *heed* your inner voice—the inner whisperings of your Higher Self that connect you to the nonvisible. Your intuition is centered in your solar plexus chakra—the energy center about an inch below your navel. Webster's dictionary defines *intuition* as "knowledge acquired without use of rational process or rational meaning based on reason." Yet, from a spiritual standpoint, intuition is *very* rational and reasonable.

God has equipped us with a spiritual umbilical cord that plugs in right below our navel, the seat of our intuition, to assist us in our journey through life. Our intuition provides us with instant knowing. Have you ever said, "Something told me . . . ," or "I had a gut feeling . . ."? This *something* isn't abstract, it's your connection to the Creator, your inner knowing that transcends the visible. Your "spiritual antenna" was communicating to you. I believe that your intuition tunes you in to places beyond the intellect. The more you trust and heed it, the more fine-tuned it gets. Messages from your intuition may show up as gut-level red flags—unexplained uneasiness or anxiety—or they can show up as gut-level green flags—unexplained feelings of certainty or rightness—depending on the situation.

I thank the Creator for equipping me with such a magnificent, exquisite extra sense. We must acknowledge that we have more than just the five "recognized" senses of sight, hearing, taste, smell, and touch. Let's change our language and start saying "the *six* senses of sight, hearing, taste, smell, touch, and intuition."

The need for constant inner renewal is closely tied to connecting to and actively using your intuition. When your gut communicates with you, listen and heed it. If your intuitive urgings go unheeded long enough, they can turn into ulcers and stomachaches—some of the results of neglecting our intuitive guidance. These dis-eases are indicators that we are possibly stifling or ignoring our intuitive communications, and in turn creating dis-ease in our bodies.

The American culture has an extreme obsession with physical things. It follows that, collectively, our intuition is grossly overlooked and underdeveloped. Many painful and costly experiences could be avoided if we acknowledged our intuition. *And* if we were *obedient* to it. Intuition plugs us into our Higher Selves—the God/ Goddess-in-us, the divine consciousness that fills us and connects us to the Creator.

If you are feeling off balance or unfocused, your connection to your intuition may need to be strengthened. You may continually be ignoring or missing the messages it's been sending, or you may not be obeying its urgings. Since life is about continual growth, I believe that intuition is part of our divine guidance system. Intuition goes beyond listening with our ears to a higher, more refined level of listening with our whole body. Our bodies are like tuning forks. They respond to the visible and the nonvisible, the heard and the unheard, the tangible and the nontangible.

But you want to be able to distinguish your intuition from the ongoing stream of self-talk and inner dialogue that seems to run on incessantly in your head. Intuition is centered in your lower stomach area, while your mental self-talk is centered in your head. Self-talk goes on at length. Intuition communicates a complete message in an instant. Our intuition becomes a stronger presence in our lives as we acknowledge it and then obey its urgings.

I've used my intuition in many ways—to help me choose my business name, Masterminds; to decide upon which college to attend when I was in a dilemma; to choose my daughter Adera's name; and in business decisions. Your intuition may even communicate to you through a dream, when your conscious mind is off duty.

In the love relationships seminars I lead around the country, I urge women to heed their heart, their head, *and* their gut when it comes to making Divine Mate (marriage) decisions. The heart represents love and passion, the head represents rational thinking, and the gut represents intuition. I suggest they heed all three.

Several particularly memorable instances come to mind as I reflect on the value of heeding my intuition. I use it ongoingly in my business, my marriage, and my personal relationships. A few years ago I had a long-awaited business meeting with two bank department directors to discuss the possibility of the bank using my training and consulting services. About an hour and a half before the appointment I received an intuitive message as I sat eating lunch at a restaurant. The message told me to prepare a specific type of training outline before I went to the meeting. I thought to myself, *No way, I'm in the middle of lunch, and I'm already prepared for this meeting. I don't have any such type of outline developed yet, and I don't have enough time to get one done before the meeting anyway.*

This meeting had been scheduled weeks in advance, and in the interim I had had a conversation with one of the bank directors to get a clear sense of the objective of the meeting and exactly what I needed to bring. I felt adequately prepared for it and was equipped with all of the appropriate and necessary materials, or so I thought. I continued to debate with myself for another minute and then dismissed the idea. Another message came through, stronger this time: *Go create it right now. You are going to need it for your meeting.* This time I decided to submit. I reluctantly surrendered to my intuition, cutting my lunch short, and made my way to the nearest Kinko's, where I could rent some time on a computer to create this document. As soon as I sat down at the computer, the document started to pour forth from my fingertips onto the keyboard as if I was typing it straight from a draft copy! An hour later I had created a two-page document that outlined my banking-specific customer-service curriculum.

Just fifteen minutes into the meeting I was astounded when one of the bank directors asked if I had an outline of my customer-service curriculum, preferably one specific to the banking industry.

*   *   *

My intuition also sent me a message the night I met my husband, Joe. In June 1992 my girlfriend Cindy invited me to join her at a house party. Within the first five minutes of arriving at the party, I had scoped out the place. And in the kitchen I spotted this fine, dark honey-brown, broad-shouldered six-foot-two-inch hunk of a man chowin' down on a plate of chicken wings. A few minutes later, after introducing myself to the party host and hostess and getting acclimated, one of my favorite songs came on. I turned around, and standing right there behind me was the fine guy I had spotted in the kitchen. Without hesitation I asked him to dance.

While we were dancing, I discreetly tried to give him the once-over, starting at his feet and working my way up to his face. I was impressed. Yes, *very* impressed. Tall, handsome, clean-cut, well built. After our first dance we had a chance to sit and talk. He was not only handsome, he was also charming, attentive, and articulate. I'm a stickler for a man's teeth and hands, and I got a chance to check those out too. Nice teeth, healthy-looking gums, clean fingernails, and strong-looking hands. By the time our second dance came around, I had a wonderfully warm, comfortable, but *very* excited feeling about this man. As a matter of fact I had that kind of excited, giddy first-date kind of feeling.

During our second dance I looked up into his face and locked eyes with him for a moment. In that moment a totally consuming feeling of knowing came over me. I knew in that instant that I was going to be with this man for a long, long time. I must have had a strange, perplexed look on my face, because he asked me if I was feeling okay. I think I may have stopped dancing for a few moments and come to a complete standstill as this feeling washed over me.

My intuition was sending me a message all right. The following year I married the man I met at that party, my husband, Joe. And he is a wonderful husband, partner, and father.

Allow your intuition to become an integral part of your life. *A pampered woman is in tune with and understands that intuition is an important spiritual tool, and strives to make full use of it.*

SACRED PAMPERING PRINCIPLE FOR THE SPIRIT #6— STAYING CONNECTED

I've noticed that some common traits are shared by women whom I consider to be "in balance." These women are spiritually well grounded. They have a strong, rich relationship with the Creator and they know how to nurture the connection. This connection is very present in their flexibility, their grace under pressure, their nonjudgmental attitudes, their graciousness, their integrity, and their humility. A woman who is connected is aware that God is in *everything,* including herself. Her life perspective is that every experience she has is for her growth, no matter how rough and difficult the situation may be at the time. Connected women have the ability to remain present to the moment—in the now—and they surrender to the Flow of Life. They are less worry- and fear-driven because they have a clear sense of the divine order behind all of the experiences that occur in their lives.

Being connected means being clear on your purpose, your passion, *and* your potential, and being obedient to the personal vision God has put in your heart. It's about feeling good about prospering when you contribute your gifts, talents, and skills to the world.

Being connected means being able to ride life's turbulent periods without crashing and burning, and being able to find your center of peace when there may be chaos around you. When you are spiritually connected, you remind yourself that you may temporarily be *in* it but that you don't have to be *of* it.

Pampering is a vehicle for more closely connecting you to your Source—the Creator, the divine Spirit. The challenge is getting more connected in a culture that puts so much emphasis on material trappings, physical things, possessions, and outer appearances, all of which are temporary. Instead we should invest more of our energy in getting grounded and being in touch with our divine nature and the God/Goddess within.

To get grounded, I often sit on the ground. I'll sit on the floor in my living room instead of on the couch or in a chair. Sitting close to the ground gives me a sense of being more grounded. If your work environment allows, you may even want to try this at work. Feeling a little overwhelmed or off balance? Try sitting on the floor for a few minutes. Have a report to finish or a writing project to complete? Go ahead and work on it while you're sitting on the floor. If you really want to try something outrageous, have a meeting while sitting on the floor in a circle. It's a definite change of pace and may even spark some creativity. Sitting on the floor in a circle can also help open up lines of communication. Need to have an important conversation with your spouse? Do it while sitting on the floor.

So much of our daily activity involves only our feet touching the floor or the ground. As our culture continues to speed up and become more machine-centered, grounding ourselves is going to become increasingly important. We're out of touch with Mother

Earth, symbolically and literally. We walk down carpeted hallways, across linoleum floors, and on top of cement-covered sidewalks and streets. We're too insulated and isolated from direct contact with Mother Earth, and our spirits are suffering. We can go through an entire day and *never* set foot on a piece of earth. We sleep on beds, sit on couches, and in desk chairs and car seats, yet our butts rarely touch the ground or even the floor. This is a travesty.

Modern comforts and the conveniences of modern technology have us grossly out of touch and disconnected from ourselves and from our Source. And they dull our relationship skills. So when I'm feeling that I'm in need of grounding, I'll eat a meal sitting on the floor in my living room instead of sitting on a chair at my dining room table. Or I'll have a sisterfriend or brotherfriend over for good conversation and herbal tea, and request that we sit on the floor for more grounding.

The sisterfriend slumber parties also have a grounding effect because we lie on the floor in sleeping bags instead of a foot and a half off the floor on top of thick bed mattresses.

Staying connected is also about keeping your life "funk-free." Keeping it free of craziness, confusion, and drama. Handling misunderstandings swiftly and thoroughly; staying clear of "drama queens," "crisis addicts," and "chaos magnets"; keeping your word; being authentic; not participating in gossip; keeping up on your financial responsibilities; following up and following through; and cleaning out toxic friendships and funky situations. Toxic friends are those who don't think their lives are interesting unless something is "going down," mess is stirred up, or strife and hardships abound. As soon as they put out one fire, another one seems to start up. And the update on what's been happening in their life always seems to sound like the latest episode of *Days of Our Lives*.

"Funk-free" means you don't let things fester. Festering situations are those that have gone too long unattended and start to infect other areas of your life. Funky situations can take the form of a love relationship that you need to release yet keep hanging on to because you're afraid of being alone or of not being able to find another man; a bad work situation that has started to affect your health; a conflict between close family members that you keep letting yourself get dragged into; situations where you allow yourself to be used and abused; or secret addictions for which you don't seek help.

So how do you know if your life has gotten a little too funky? Do the following self-assessment to find out. Funkiness can be a beacon to direct you to places in your life that need some attention and cleanup work. Check those that are true for you. If any of these apply, it's time to do some mental and emotional housecleaning.

___ Your finances have been seriously messed up for a while and you haven't been doing anything about it.

___ You're tolerating verbal, mental, or physical abuse from a boyfriend, spouse, or friend.

___ Friends are falling out of your life.

___ You are constantly pissed off.

___ You "go off" on others easily.

___ Your personal appearance is deteriorating.

___ You're spending more and more time alone, and it is *not* by choice.

___ Your desk, office, or home environment is constantly messy.

___ An addiction is surfacing or resurfacing.

Funky people, situations, and relationships drain your energy, waste your time, eat away at your personal power, and block your good. Be committed to keeping your life funk-free. It helps you remain in balance.

SACRED PAMPERING PRINCIPLE FOR THE SPIRIT #7— SACRED SILENCE

Silence can be sacred. Webster's dictionary defines *silence* simply as "stillness." Within the context of nineties living, which is filled with too much motion and madness, silence can be a form of sacred stillness. For our lives to be balanced, we must incorporate blocks of silence, even if they are small blocks. Balanced living necessitates silence in order to counter the effects of sensory overload that contemporary living gives us. Silence can be a powerful remedy for many of our contemporary dysfunctions and dis-eases, such as unhappiness, lack of creativity, boredom, and lack of motivation. Silence is sacred, meaning "worthy of respect and honor." When you honor something, you don't take it for granted. But we don't honor or respect silence enough. In the course of an average day we are bombarded with noise and activity. Noises you may encounter include the buzzer on your alarm clock; running water, the bell on the microwave, the radio, stereo, conversations, yelling, sirens, loud engines, screeching tires, ringing telephones, and slamming doors. Our senses get saturated and overloaded.

Sadly enough, in our noisy, distracting society it requires effort to *integrate* silence into our lives. This is probably why we tolerate going *without* it so easily. In our high-tech, fast-paced, "instant" society (instant photo, instant gratification, and instant pain relief), silence isn't highly valued. Being alone with ourselves and our thoughts is a scary proposition for many of us.

When was the last time you enjoyed the sacredness of silence? No radio, no music playing, no television, no ringing phone, no dishwasher or washing machine running, just silence—*with yourself and by yourself.* Even for four or five minutes? Most of us cannot remember the last time. It's been that long! Removing ourselves from this sensory overload is exactly what many of us desperately need. Why is it that we have such a hard time just *BEING*—choosing *intentional solitude,* holding still, chilling out? This is a key part of self-mastery and a self-caring lifestyle, the ability to be quiet with and by yourself—*solitary refinement.* When you are silent, you can hear the whisperings of your intuition. Paying attention and deep contemplation happen in the silence. Nature's power is a silent, awesome power. Nature in all of its magnificence unfolds in the silence. Flowers bloom, trees grow, fruit ripens, ferns unfurl, seeds sprout roots, and blades of grass break through the soil stretching toward the light. And all of this happens elegantly and *quietly,* without spotlights, headlines, neon signs, or fanfare.

When I was a little girl, I would squirm around as my mama tried to press my hair. Throughout the two-hour ordeal she'd have to tell me continually to "hold still, girl." Even as an adult, in the earlier stages of my spiritual development and evolution, I found it difficult to hold still. I didn't want to miss anything. I wanted to be on the hottest tip and in the mix. After all, holding still meant that life might pass me by, right? I might miss something. I discovered that the only thing I was missing was my peace of mind.

One of my most profound realizations is that the essence of life resides *within* the stillness. Yet, I was always *in pursuit,* trying to catch it. And it would evaporate or slip out of my hands like a greased pig as soon as I thought I finally had it. I thought it was *out there,* around the next corner or across town at the hippest nightclub. All the while it was in the Present Moment. The Now. The Right Here. Right where my butt was planted.

Dwelling in silence allows you to get to know yourself better. To get to know someone, you desire to spend quality time with him or her. Yet we don't spend quality time with *ourselves!* How can we expect others to invest in quality time with us if we don't have the discipline or commitment to spend quality time with ourselves? Something is wrong with this picture. If you can't enjoy your own company in silence and be comfortable and at ease with yourself, how can you expect others to? Yet we continue to have this expectation, don't we?

To start incorporating more silence into your life, you can begin right where you are, with the simple things. For example, reading in silence, writing a poem, drawing, bathing, deep breathing, touching, massaging, praying, journaling, and creative thinking. Notice over the next three days what activities and experiences you can shift to doing in silence. Build silence into your lifestyle. We should begin instituting daily Family Moments of Silence, too. It would transform this country. Have the entire household honor silence together for five minutes a day. Pause for a few minutes of silent grace before your family eats a meal. Designate a half hour one night a week for Sacred Silent Time for the entire family. Reading, journaling, creative thinking, prayer, meditation, and nightly silent time are a few ways I integrate silence into my lifestyle. Record the differences that you notice.

I have yet to talk to a participant in one of my seminars and workshops who started incorporating more silence into her life and it *didn't* make a difference. Though my oldest daughter, Adera, is only three years old, I'm already starting to teach her the value of silence. Periodically I'll have her sit beside me on the floor in front of my altar with her head bowed for a few minutes of silence. Right now she is only able to hold still for a few minutes without getting fidgety, but I'm working on building her up to a full five minutes. To help them get used to the notion of Quiet Time, in the mornings she and Kiana, who is two years old, know to stay in their room playing quietly.

Have you noticed how the American culture seems to have invested a lot in keeping us distracted, in motion, and on the go? Our days are filled with various kinds of activities that keep us always moving and *doing*. We turn off the TV when we leave the house. We get in the car to go to work and we turn on the radio. We get to work and turn off the car and the radio and then we turn on the computer. We turn off the computer, drive home, and then turn on the stove, TV, or dishwasher. Many stores are open seven days a week. Sundays have started to resemble the other six days of the week—filled with hustle and bustle. Restaurants and nightclubs that are open around-the-clock are becoming more commonplace. And twenty-four-hour TV programming is standard. Enough already! Why do we keep running from silence? We're perpetuating a cycle of overstimulation, sensory overload, and mental anxiety that keeps moving us farther and farther from our inner core. What are we trying to avoid?

Silence enables us to get in touch with our inner self, where the God/Goddess-within-us dwells. Possibly the investment in keeping us overstimulated and distracted comes from a deep fear of us getting in touch with the Source of our personal power—the essence of God/Goddess that dwells within—beating our hearts, endowing us with the ability to love, and enabling our bodies to self-heal.

As you continue to incorporate silence into your life, you will increasingly get in touch with your Source. Maybe the fear is that if we get in touch with the reality that we each are *co-creators* with God/Goddess, we might realize the power of our minds. We might discover that we can heal our bodies completely, eliminate lack and limitation, fear, poverty, and racism. We might realize that we each *create and attract* our experiences and realities, not the media—MTV, BET, Warner Bros., *Vogue, Cosmopolitan,* or *Ebony.*

In examining why there isn't more silence in our lives, we also have to take a look at the impact of technology. In my view technolgy is both a blessing and a curse. We can microwave a potato in ten minutes instead of baking it for sixty. Yet do we take this saved fifty minutes and immerse ourselves in a pampering bath or indulge in Solitary Refinement? Heck, no! We go and fill it up with more stuff, "busy-ness," and activity!

When I lived in Los Angeles after graduating from college, I started to notice how being constantly "busy" was considered cool. It was rare to call someone and speak to a live, warm body instead of an answering machine. Everyone was always out doing *something*. Being busy was definitely "in." But all this constant *doing* and busyness for the sake of being able to say that you were doing something was obsessive. Though southern California had a laid-back image, the reality was that folks were uptight and on edge. Constant busyness with no silence leads to restlessness, loss of focus, and emptiness.

So to get on track and stay on track requires that we redesign our lives with daily silence as a necessary, uncompromised ingredient. I suggest starting with five minutes of silence a day and working your way up from there. Five minutes may sound like a breeze, but try it for an entire week and see how you do. Pay attention to how easy and comfortable, or difficult and uncomfortable it is for you. Do you feel compelled to be doing something else more "constructive"? Do you feel as if you are wasting time? Are you fidgety? Are you relaxed? Is your mental chatter going nonstop? Do all of the things you "should" be doing start creeping into your head, or are you present to each moment? Is your mind wandering off to the housework that needs to be done or the things at the office you need to complete? For some of us incorporating even five minutes of silence into our daily living can be a challenge. Silence enables us to commune with God, to indulge in spiritual fellowship with the Goddess-in-us, to connect with our true selves.

Sacred Pampering Principle for the Spirit #8—
Tapping the Goddess Within

We can learn a lot about ourselves from examining our indigenous African spirituality. A common trait you will notice that also runs through other ancient indigenous cultures of color is that *both* the masculine and the feminine aspects of the Creator are acknowledged and represented in the language and images. The male and female principles show up in the ancient Chinese concept of yang and yin, the goddess Shakti and the god Shiva in the Hindu culture, Ausar and Auset in the Egyptian Khamitic culture, Father Sky and Mother Earth in the Native American cultures, and the male and female orishas of the West African Yoruba religion.

Western-European religions, however, do not have a balance of the masculine and feminine principles. We've received images that represent God as a patriarchal masculine image, denying the feminine aspect of the Creator altogether. I don't think we're fully aware of the damage these heavily patriarchal images have done to our minds. The result is suppression of the Feminine within ourselves, represented by the Goddess.

Just like the Western-European images that exalt the Masculine to the exclusion of the Feminine in their representations of the Creator, our masculine energies have tended to be overdeveloped while our feminine energies have remained underdeveloped. I think this especially applies to us as African-American women. Our history in this country shows that in order to survive, we've had to keep putting our masculine selves forward while our feminine selves have had to take a backseat. So now our masculine and feminine energies are out of balance. It's time to tone down the Masculine and allow our Feminine to flourish again. When we don't nurture and pamper ourselves enough, which helps to bring out the balancing feminine aspects of our being, we tend to get overmasculinized. To help you get clear on these feminizing aspects, it is useful to look at the qualities represented by the Goddess, the feminine aspect of the Creator.

The essential qualities of the Goddess are represented by openness, softness, contemplation, nurturing, feeling, receiving, listening, intuition, poise, tranquillity, gracefulness, composure, rest, and knowing. The God energy, the masculine energy, is represented by activity, achieving, thinking, speaking, reason, action, and doing. Our overmasculinization shows up in many ways: being too loud, hard, forceful, mean, dominating, and controlling. You'll notice that Western culture's values as a whole lean heavily toward masculine approaches and styles. We've been stuck in a mode and a mind-set that suppresses the Goddess energy, and it is time to return to a state of balance.

Western culture and its masculinized images combined with the remnants of the Mammie and Aunt Jemima images of the "consummate caregiver" from slavery have done some serious psychic and spiritual damage to Black women. These dynamics have had the effect of forcing Black women into "masculinized" postures. Mammie and Aunt Jemima were masculinized, nonfeminine images. The images represented the overworked Black woman who didn't need to rest, relax, receive, or pamper herself. She was portrayed as being content with taking care of everyone else but herself, all while suppressing and negating the feminine aspects of her being.

These images, which are reminiscent in our modern-day TV sitcoms and movies, are very powerful because they are absorbed by our psyches as little girls and then reinforced as grown women. Remember the loud-talking, Bible-totin', purse-swingin' Aunt Esther from *Sanford and Son*? The sassy, abrasive maid, Florence, from *The Jeffersons*? Or sharp-tongued, angry Pam from *Martin*? A couple of these shows are off the air, but you probably still recall the images from each of these examples.

So what are the indicators that your feminine energies may be suppressed and out of balance? Here are a few: incessant "busyness," lack of thorough and adequate rest, anger toward men, blaming men for your feelings of powerlessness, the Strong Black Woman Syndrome, being overly self-sufficient, not allowing contribution or assistance from others, steadily giving but not receiving, a sharp tongue, harsh words, loud talking, cursing.

The suppression of our feminine energies also manifests in our bodies as dis-eases that centralize in our female organs. When the feminine aspects of our being are not expressed outwardly, they become suppressed, turn negative, and seek expression inwardly. Denial of the feminine aspects of yourself can lead to the harboring of negative, toxic thoughts and emotions. Deeply buried self-hatred and resentment of others, especially men, can start to build. These negative, suppressed energies continue to put stress on your system until they implode like a shaken bottle of soda. Accumulated negative energies weaken your system and create vulnerabilities within it—and for Black women our most weakened areas tend to be our feminine organs—breasts, ovaries, vagina, uterus, and cervix. When the implosion occurs, our feminine organs manifest dis-ease, usually in the form of cancer, fibroids, or cysts. Notice how the incidence of cancer of the cervix, breasts, and uterus has sharply risen in the last decade among Black women, and the occurrence of ovarian or uterine cysts and fibroids has been on the rapid increase as well!!

It is time for us to soften up and allow our feminine energies to emerge. Goddess energy is neither inferior nor superior to God energy—it is a balancing complement to it. Self-care is a way to bring your masculine and feminine energies back into balance.

SACRED PAMPERING PRINCIPLE FOR THE SPIRIT #9— GOING WITH THE FLOW

When we keep bumping our heads into the same walls and setbacks, when we keep struggling or expending too much effort and energy, we aren't going with the Flow. Life has a natural flow to it, like a river. We experience what we call problems when we're fighting or resisting the Flow. When we dig in our heels trying to do it *our* way, trying to control and micro-manage every detail, we are not going with the Flow. Instead of being aligned with the Creator's agenda for our lives, we keep trying to assert our own agenda. We become like salmon trying to swim upstream, and life becomes *hard.* Life's Flow always moves you onward, upward, and forward. So when you're feel as if you're slipping backward, downward, or going nowhere, it's because you're fighting the Flow.

When you're going *with* the Flow, you're not focused on the details, you're focused on the outcome. You hold the intention and the vision and you let the Creator handle the details of the *how.*

When you're going with the Flow, you are present to every part of the journey because you know that the Flow is moving you toward your Higher Good. But instead of submitting to the Flow, we kick, fight, scream, and complain. Then we wonder why life is so difficult. When we're constantly spinning our wheels, sabotaging ourselves, or taking two steps backward for every step forward, it is usually because we need to *let go, detach ourselves from the outcome,* and learn to trust, have faith, release, and *move over so that Providence can move in.*

Part of going with the Flow is getting clear on the outcome and *allowing* the Creator to handle the *how* of it. Often we put too much energy into the How instead of getting crystal-clear on the What. In order for the contract between me and the publisher for this book to come about, a series of divine connections and intersections occurred. I kept holding the *vision* and I let God be the *provision.* As a little girl I'd envisioned seeing my book on the shelves of bookstores across the country. This vision remained clear in my mind over the years, even when *Sacred Pampering Principles* was still in its self-published form. I stayed focused on the vision and I let the Creator handle the details of the How. Remember, going with the Flow isn't about giving up, it's about giving it *over* to the Creator.

In the American culture we are obsessed with having certainty and minimizing the risk. We try to predict, dissect, and analyze everything to death in hopes of removing the uncertainty, instead of trusting the deliberate, underlying divine order that emerges when you detach, lift your heels, and go with the Flow. When things aren't flowing, we must stop and ask ourselves, "What is it that I'm avoiding or resisting? What outcome am I afraid of experiencing? What is the message in this that supports my continued growth? What is the lesson in this that I need to get?"

After leaving AT&T in southern California, where I worked for a couple of years after graduating from college, I returned to Washington State to work in my parents' telecommunications company. After a couple of years I became restless. The thoughts I had been stifling, about starting my own business, started to resurface. Each time these thoughts came up, I'd stifle them again. They created conflict within me because I felt obligated to support my parents by working in the family business; after all they'd sacrificed for me. After the first three years these thoughts of starting my own full-time training and consulting business began to resurface more frequently. I started feeling less committed, less enthusiastic, and less focused each day. My productivity started to drop. Going to work every day felt like a chore. I allowed this inner battle to continue for another year before I mustered up enough courage to take action. It was time for me to move on, but I was fighting the Flow.

The Flow was trying to move me on, but I was afraid. Afraid of the consequences. I didn't fully trust my gifts, talents, skills, and abilities as a trainer and consultant, *and* I had feelings of guilt about leaving. But the truth of the matter was that I also liked the security of receiving a paycheck every month. So what was keeping me from not being true to myself was the triple threat of self-doubt, guilt, and insecurity, the three great enemies of positive action, faith, and forward motion. I had my heels dug *deep* into my comfort zone. I was resisting the Flow.

One of the powerful lessons I learned through this process is that the Creator is so committed to our continuous growth and evolution that She will kick our butts to get us moving if She has to. If you are not taking action where you know you need to be, you may get a spiritual whack upside the head. And this whack may be in the form of a layoff, termination, or a perfect opportunity. Soon thereafter I found out that I was pregnant with our second child. This seemed like a sign to me. With a second child now on the way I *had* to make a decision. Was I going to return to work after my three months of maternity leave, or was I going to step out on faith and start my training and consulting business? I decided that it was finally time for me to step out.

When we allow fear to creep in instead of trusting the process, trusting ourselves, trusting the Creator, and trusting the Flow, we strangle miracles, stifle creativity, and miss out on the fullness of our blessings. The more we resist, the more emotional, spiritual, and mental logjams we create. Logjams block the Flow and reduce our stream of Good to a trickle. Our fear erects an impassable dam and releases poisonous contaminants into the Flow. These contaminants may be doubt, insecurity, deeply buried self-hatred, and thoughts of lack, limitation, and failure.

It is now time for us to release the tight-fisted, viselike grips we've had on our passion, prosperity, gifts, creativity, talents, joy, and love. Many of us are clogged, blocked, and spiritually constipated. Pampering is Ex-Lax for the spirit. It assists us in going with the Flow—"letting go and letting God."

SACRED PAMPERING PRINCIPLE FOR THE SPIRIT #10— FOLLOWING YOUR BLISS

Bliss is a state of ecstasy or joy. I think we were intended to live blissfully and joyfully. However, many of us have a serious "joy shortage" in our lives. Our lives are not organized around what brings us joy, but instead around what brings us security, certainty, health benefits, or a steady paycheck. We need a new blueprint for living that is organized and prioritized around what brings us joy. So much of our lives have been defined by outside forces, whether it be our parents, the educational system, the media, social expectations, peers, or cultural norms. It becomes easy to get out of touch with your Bliss. When you are following your Bliss, you are doing what brings you joy and allows you to fully express and contribute your gifts, talents, skills, and abilities to the world.

When you are following your Bliss, you don't need an alarm clock to wake you up in the morning. You get absorbed in what you are doing and time seems to fly. Your creativity flows, and you are turned on about what you are doing. Following your Bliss in your work is when you choose to do work you enjoy. When you are moving in the groove of your life purpose, you are living a life aligned with your Bliss. Each of our lives takes the necessary twists and turns to keep us on track for our personal purpose. Even though it may appear at times as though we are lost. Even what appears to be off track is part of the journey and the process. So be patient with yourself.

My two-and-a-half-year experience in corporate America was part of my "track." At first corporate America was new and exciting.

I was like a wide-eyed kid in a candy store. The challenge and the competitive environment energized me. I jumped in headfirst and kicked butt. My first year at AT&T I had become one of the top account executives in the country. I hadn't planned on bumping my head against the proverbial glass ceiling so soon, though.

After two years of being a top performer, I started having to force myself to get motivated. I was no longer on a natural high. The excitement had faded and turned into effort. The corporate scene was getting to me—the competitive atmosphere, the obsession with meeting quotas and getting more sales, the office politics, the pressure to conform, having to report to work at eight A.M. every day—all of it was getting to me. There were days I just didn't feel like putting on the nylons, the heels, and the suits. Sometimes I didn't want to have to play by someone else's rules. Sometimes I wanted to sleep in. Sometimes I didn't want my actions to be dictated by corporate politics, fragile egos, and jockeying for promotions. I was tired of having to meet and exceed sales quotas month after month, upholding the reputation of being a top producer. It started feeling like a grind, and I knew it was time for me to "graduate" from AT&T and move on. I was suffocating.

I had to take a step back and determine what would really bring me joy. I started by creating a profile of a work environment that would be the best fit for me. This is what I came up with: I needed freedom of self-expression and creativity. I wanted to be able to work *with* the grain of my personal rhythm, instead of against it—which meant not getting up until nine or nine-thirty if I chose, and working late at night. I wanted the flexibility to take longer lunches and to have my day integrated with periods of relaxation. I wanted the latitude to think "outside of the box" and play by different rules instead of having to conform to the status quo. I wanted to work four days a week, not five.

I held on to this vision. I continued to have patience with the process. I was committed to having a work style in line with my vision someday. I stayed focused on the vision and I let the Creator handle the provision. Now, five years later, this vision is a reality.

I've created an environment and work tempo that allow my passion and joy to flourish and for my skills, talents, gifts, and abilities to be fully utilized. Masterminds, my training and consulting firm, is the vehicle that created the fit I was looking for. Getting to this point required faith, perseverance, and patience with my process. And I now realize that my path through AT&T and my parent's company was not a detour, it was a necessary part of my journey.

In order to design your lifework around your Bliss, you must first know what kind of life brings you joy. You must *define it and design it*. Create an inner image, a vision in full color and sound, complete with smell, taste, and texture. Make it real in your mind, write it down in vivid detail, and do not let go of the vision. What does your day consist of? What is the tempo of your week? What gifts, talents, skills, and abilities are you putting to use?

One of my discoveries about the power of following your Bliss is that it transforms the quality of your entire life. Following your Bliss is a holistic approach to living because it is the expression of your Total Self—mind, body, and spirit. But because we are each evolving at different rates, manifesting a life that reflects our Bliss occurs at different times for each of us. We are not in competition with anyone else. Personal growth has a personal frame of reference. We move along according to our own rate of growth and development. For some of us it may not manifest until we are forty-one, fifty-one, or sixty-one. For others it may be at age twenty-seven or thirty-one.

Metaphorically, following your Bliss is like the process of gardening. The vision is the fruit we plan to bear. Once we plant the seed of the vision, we must cultivate the seed by watering, nurturing, and cultivating it. Cultivation of our vision comes in the form of doing the spiritual work, applying the faith, positive action, and patience that fertilizes the seed of the vision and enables it to ripen into fruit.

SACRED PAMPERING PRINCIPLE FOR THE SPIRIT #11— AN ATTITUDE OF GRATITUDE

For the most part we take the gracious actions of others for granted. We act as if we are entitled, as if someone's helping or supporting us, or even simply returning a phone call, is behavior to be expected instead of a gift and a privilege. Expressing gratitude is a function of being humble, having an attitude of gratitude, and a prosperity consciousness. It is also in line with spiritual law: What goes around comes around. You reap what you sow. A pampered woman strives to develop a consciousness of prosperity and abundance. She understands that being grateful and expressing thanks keeps her blessings flowing. She understands that what she sows with her attitudes and behaviors she will eventually reap. A self-caring woman is constantly looking for opportunities to express gratitude.

I was able to make great strides with my new training and consulting business in a short period of time because I decided to build my business upon a cornerstone of gratitude. I expressed thanks for every referral, introduction, returned phone call, contract signed, or time taken out to have lunch or coffee with me. In the first nine months of my new business I sent out more thank-you cards than I had, cumulatively, in my entire life. In turn an amazing and unexpected result occurred. In that same nine-month period I *received* more thank-you cards, notes, and letters of gratitude from clients, associates, friends, and workshop participants than I had received over the past nine years! In addition I was able to build my business and secure the kinds of impressive contracts that "veteran" consultants usually secured.

Gratitude requires that you acknowledge your blessing and treat others and their actions as *gifts*. Expressing and demonstrating gratitude and thanks widens your receiving conduit. Giving and receiving work in partnership. Each is a function of the other. Being grateful and thankful is *a posture, an attitude, a disposition*. It is a posture grounded in thankfulness and appreciation.

The Bible is filled with verses that emphasize the importance of an attitude of gratitude. In 1 Thessalonians 5:18, the Bible says, "We are to give thanks in everything." Ephesians 1:16 encourages us to "cease not giving thanks," and Ephesians 5:20 says, "Give thanks always." Giving thanks opens the doors to many blessings. We are continuously instructed to give thanks in the Bible. And it even goes as far as to cite specific instances in which we should most certainly give thanks—during private prayer, during public worship, upon completing a great undertaking, before eating, for wisdom, for deliverance from adversity, for faith exhibited *by others,* for love exhibited *by others,* for grace bestowed *on others,* for the nearness of the Creator's presence, for supply of our bodily wants, and when giving an offering.

Shifting to a posture of gratitude has been a gradual process for me, and the blessings have come in abundance. In addition to receiving exotic and colorful thank-you cards, letters, and notes, I've also received more gifts and tokens of appreciation over these last three years than in any other three-year period in my life. And I am clear that it is a direct effect of shifting to an attitude of *conscious gratitude.* In Mark 4:20 the Bible discusses how sowing seeds on good ground brings forth good fruit. I believe an attitude of gratitude helps you cultivate "good ground." When the seeds of our daily actions, decisions, and choices are planted in the "good ground" of gratitude, appreciation, and humility, we reap fruit a hundredfold, as it says in Luke 8:8.

I'm always trying to be alert to opportunities for expressing thanks to others—even if it's having my gas pumped at a full-service gas station and saying "Thank you!" to the attendant. Yes, I pay a premium for having my gas pumped for me at a full-serve station, but full-service gas stations are so rare these days that I really appreciate being able to have someone else do it for me, especially on a rainy day. I've even sent thank-you cards to reporters who do a good job on a newspaper story about me because I realize that an inaccurate media story can be very damaging. I also try to give thanks to a friendly salesperson, a helpful customer-service representative, and a cheerful receptionist. Start right now, this moment, giving thanks. Thank the Creator for the eyes that enable you to read these words. Thank the Creator for the breath you are taking in right this moment. Thank the Creator for the shelter that is over your head. Whisper those thanks to yourself right now. . . .

As you go about your day, look for ways to express gratitude. During the day when a friend is at work, call her home answering machine and leave a loving message; when you are paying for groceries at the cash register checkout, ask your checker, "How are you doing today?"; hold the door open for others; clip out a newspaper or magazine article that you think may interest a business associate and mail it to her; give an extra tip to a cheerful waiter or waitress; rather than using the traditional closing of "sincerely" on your letters and cards, use "gratefully yours" instead; wave to acknowledge your appreciation when someone lets you go ahead of them in traffic; or treat a friend to lunch.

To show my appreciation to a group of sisterfriends who attended a special pampering party I gave at my house, I presented each of them with a book from my personal library. Once in a while I'll call a girlfriend and start singing the first few words of the chorus of Stevie Wonder's song "I Just Called to Say I Love You." Look for opportunities to say, "I appreciate . . ." and "Thank you for . . ." You never know how an attitude of gratitude might brighten someone's day, or your own! Give a compliment to a stranger. Write "thank you!" in the memo section of your checks or on the outside of your bill envelopes before mailing them.

If you give thanks with a willing, open heart, the blessings will pour forth.

SACRED PAMPERING PRINCIPLE FOR THE SPIRIT #12— ACHIEVING A BALANCED LIFE

When you do something that is a *demonstration* of self-love, then, it also becomes an act of loving yourself. Thus pampering not only *leads* you to greater self-love, but it also acts as the stepping-stones on the path itself. Pampering brings equilibrium to your life. Little by little, as you start to organize your life around more self-supporting priorities, healthier choices, and self-care first, your life starts to reflect more balance. One of the magical qualities of pampering is that it is both the journey and the destination simultaneously. When you are pampering yourself, your appreciation and love of self inch forward and upward with each pampering experience.

Setting Healthy Boundaries

A key ingredient to achieving balance is setting and maintaining healthy boundaries for yourself. Set boundaries about how, where, on what and with whom you use your energy. Pampering helps bring balance to life because it counters and neutralizes those things that drain your power, steal your joy, and wear you down. It revitalizes your spirit and helps you know where to draw the line. Draw it based on your priorities, maintaining peace of mind, protecting your energy, and your commitment to your mental, spiritual, physical, and emotional needs first.

Here's a little quiz to help you assess how you're doing so far with setting healthy boundaries. Give yourself one point for each yes answer. A yes answer means that the statement is true for you *most* of the time.

— You say yes when you really want to say no.

— You overcommit your time.

— You are worn out from nurturing others.

— You are good at fulfilling others' requests, but you're not good at making them, especially when it comes to asking for help, assistance, or nurturing from others.

— You say yes to doing things out of guilt, obligation, or expectations.

— You constantly rush getting ready in the morning.

— You don't allow yourself enough transition time, travel or preparation time between meetings, appointments, projects, or clients.

— You wait until the last minute.

— You're overly critical of yourself.

— You're overworked.

— You're overweight.

— You are heavily dependent on others' opinions or advice.

— Your life is filled with activity, but you are not "fullfilled."

— You don't allow adequate time for daily personal grooming.

— Your body has frequent minor aches and pains.

— You consistently attract drama and crisis into your life in periodic cycles.

Now go back and total up your points. Each yes is one point. The good news is that I'm not going to give you a rating scale. Your objective is to decrease your point total, with your ultimate goal being to achieve a 0 score.

The purpose of the exercise is to increase your awareness of current dynamics in your life that call attention to areas that are possibly contributing to imbalances. When you are presented with a situation or a request that you want to decline, work on using phrases that will assist you in doing it firmly and without guilt. Setting healthy boundaries requires that you learn to say *guiltlessly*, "That doesn't work for me," or "No, thank you," or "I'll pass." Healthy boundaries help you protect your energy and use it wisely—for the things and with the people that you want to.

Pacing

Pacing is a very important part of achieving balance in your life. Pacing is about discovering your unique tempo—your personal rhythm. Each of us has a life rhythm that works for us. Some of us have a tolerance and threshold for a faster pace than others. The key is to stay with a self-dictated pace that works for you. Your life may be whizzing along at ninety-five miles per hour and you need to slow it down to sixty-five. You may need to cut something out of your schedule, let something go, or decide not to participate. Use the following question as a yardstick for assessing what should stay and what should go in your life: *Is this activity/relationship/situation contributing positively to my mental, emotional, and spiritual health?*

Finding my own pace and organizing my life around this pace has been a process that has required patience. And one of the amazing ironies of living my life according to a self-dictated pace is that I am able to fit it all in—my husband, my little girls, my work, my speaking engagements, homemaking, movement, relaxation, friendships, and pampering. It is amazing how a "self-care first" lifestyle enables you to have it all with ease and grace. When you are better taken care of, you are better able to see to the other important people and activities in your life.

I work at living the very prescriptions and processes set forth in this book, living what I'm teaching. And it's taken me about four years to get my life to a point of balance and integrated self-care. I realize that when I am pampered, rested, and revitalized, I am more relaxed, happier, patient, and productive. I am mentally and emotionally more present, energetic, loving, tolerant, understanding, humorous, and focused when I'm in balance and maintaining my self-dictated life tempo. But believe me, it is an ongoing process, much like climbing a mountain that has no top. And along the way you may slip and lose your foothold temporarily. That's okay. Take a deep breath. Relax. Recenter yourself, and keep pressing toward the mark.

Yes, it is possible to have it all without having to be Superwoman. Superwoman didn't realize that the answer was *not* in trying to stuff and squeeze *more* activity into her already full life. What she was missing was a new paradigm for being able to have it all without having to wear herself down and wear herself out. What was missing in *her* paradigm was a different perspective, a new vantage point, a new order of priorities where *self-care comes first.* She was trying to stuff and squeeze more in, while self-care remained at the bottom of her Priority Pole as her lowest priority. Now the truth is out, and the truth shall set you free! Living your life with a self-care-first approach makes space for all that is important for you. And your life takes on more depth and quality. Care of self first isn't selfish, it's necessary, and *it's smart!*

Making Space in Your Life

Achieving balance requires that you make space in your life. This includes your physical spaces too. Your bedroom, car, closets, purse, desk, and cabinets. When these places get cluttered, it's usually because they are a reflection of our minds, which are also too full and cluttered. So we need to do some mental and emotional housecleaning to free up some space. Often our lives are cluttered and crowded with unhealthy relationships and obligations that consume our time but don't enrich our spirits or touch our hearts. We stay in friendships where there's not enough reciprocity. There's too much effort and struggle and very little positive return. We stay in love relationships where the love is gone. We have friends who can easily wallow in our woe but don't want to participate in our victories. Our calendars are filled with activities that don't forward us. Our styles are too cramped. We've been doing the same things the same way for far too long and it's time for a change. *We need to make some space* to spread out, to breathe, to be freer.

I try to spring-clean my life physical spaces at least twice a year. Some of the ways I make space are to clean out my purse and wallet, clear off the patio, or clean out my closet. I get rid of any clothes in my closets and drawers I haven't worn over the past twelve months. We need to stop hanging on to clothes that no longer fit us. If we haven't worn them or used them in the past twelve months, then give them up. Have a garage sale. Give them to a girlfriend. Donate the items to the Salvation Army or a homeless women's shelter. When we create more space in our physical places, it gives us more mental and spiritual space in our lives. We need to clean it up where it's gotten messy. Where it's gotten complicated, we need to simplify. Give it away if we're not using it. Give it up if we don't want it anymore. But *make some space!*

You must understand that you are the magnet in your life. *You are the common denominator in all of your experiences.* You are a *living, breathing magnet*—attracting specific people, circumstances, and situations into your life moment to moment. So we have to stop and take inventory once in a while. If we're personally out of balance, so are the people and situations we're attracting. When we're out of balance, we tend *not* to do things that bring us joy. More joy can't come into your life unless there's some *room* for it.

4

SACRED PAMPERING
PRINCIPLES FOR THE BODY

Your body is your divine packaging. You only get one this lifetime around. No trade-ins. No exchanges. Yet we treat our bodies
as if the one we are born with is a practice model. We act like our
new body is going to arrive any minute. Like this body is for a test
run. Why is it we have such a hard time fully accepting our bodies
and all of our body parts just as they are? We still have parts of
our bodies that we haven't accepted, really don't like, or would
replace if it were possible. We are stuck in the "If Only" Syndrome.

When you get stuck in the "If Only" Syndrome, full self-acceptance
of your physical body is based on an ideal or an "if only" condition.
"Once my slimmer body gets here, I'll start being more outgoing
with men." "Once my slimmer body gets here, I'll start taking better
care of myself." And the "If Only" Syndrome also has you thinking
thoughts like "If only my hair would grow . . . If only my skin were
clearer . . . If only my thighs were slimmer . . . If only my butt
were smaller. . . . The "If Only" Syndrome can put your life on
hold or keep you stuck in a state of stagnation. Many of us feel as

if we are in bondage in our bodies. We are secretly waiting for a new body to get here so that we can *really* start living.

As Black women, if we leave it up to the mainstream culture and media, we will never be okay in the African-style bodies we are born with. The shoes aren't sized or designed with our wider foot in mind. The jeans aren't cut with our broader hips in mind. The bras aren't shaped with our fuller breasts in mind. The shampoos aren't created with our curlier hair in mind. Yet subconsciously we continue to hold cruel yardsticks up to ourselves, silently comparing our dimensions, shapes, and sizes to that of the dominant culture. And within *their* context our bodies are not okay.

In a Personal Power seminar I led in St. Louis, I asked women to share what parts of their bodies they were not at peace with, the parts they really didn't like and would change if they could. The very parts of their bodies that were naturally fuller, wider, or rounder were the parts *least* embraced—breasts, butts, noses, hips, feet, and stomachs!

Where else does the notion of only partial physical self-acceptance come from if it doesn't originate from some kind of unhealthy comparison against a standard? *So why do we continue putting ourselves through this agony and suffering?* We can no longer let the mainstream culture define or determine what body image we consider acceptable for us. It is damaging to our body image and sense of self.

The inner battle that rages around our body-acceptance issues is a result of the continual attempt to convince ourselves that we're okay while society's messages and advertisements bombard us daily with images that tell us otherwise. Our partial acceptance of our bodies shows up in more ways than just the covering up and disguising that we do. I made out a list that answered this question: What parts of my body do I have the hardest time accepting, *as is, right now?* I was shocked to discover that there weren't many parts of my body that I *did* accept as is. At the time I first did this exercise, my list went something like this: my teeth, my stomach, my butt, my hips, my thighs, my knees, and my feet. My list didn't leave much that *was* okay.

You may laugh at a few of these entries, but I had real issues with each one at the time. In my opinion my teeth had a slight gap, and I was conscious of the cap on my left front tooth; my fingernails were too short; my stomach wasn't flat enough; my butt was too big; my hips were too wide; my thighs jiggled; I had knock-knees; and my toes had corns on them. And at the time I considered myself to be a woman who really loved and embraced herself and her body.

There are things we do to our bodies that demonstrate that we have a big problem with body acceptance. These include being overweight, overeating, smoking, taking drugs, and overdrinking. It is time for us to come to loving terms with our bodies. The way we reconcile this inner conflict in our minds, which then shows up in our bodies, is by compensating for these feelings of bodily inadequacy by covering up or disguising those parts of our bodies that we don't really like. And parts of your body that you don't like are like carrying around pieces of self-hatred in your psyche.

What are the areas of your body you are covering up or disguising? Use the area below to list specific parts of your body that you've been hiding or camouflaging. What areas are in need of more embracing and acceptance?

◈ _____   ◈ _____
◈ _____   ◈ _____
◈ _____   ◈ _____
◈ _____   ◈ _____

We spend amazing amounts of time, energy, and money findings ways to camouflage our bodily "inadequacies."

Sacred Pampering Principle for the Body #1— Your Body Temple

Being at home in your body is what this principle is about. It goes beyond being comfortable *with* your body to being comfortable *in* your body. This is an important distinction to make. If you are at home in your body, being comfortable with it follows.

The Bible, in all of its wisdom, in 1 Corinthians 3:16–17, teaches us that our bodies are temples of God, where the Spirit of the living God dwells. It goes on to say that the temple is not to be defiled. As a temple of God we each are holy, because the temple of God is holy. The word *holy* means "belonging to or associated with a divine power."

We know, however, that there are times where our bodies don't *feel* holy or *look* holy to us. These are the times when we cover up and disguise our bodies, neglect our bodies, or abuse them with improper food or bad habits. I think one of our greatest accomplishments in life is to arrive at the place where we see our bodies as divine temples and treat them as such, just as they are.

Your body is a divine creation, intentionally and lovingly designed to take you through this earthly lifetime. The standard that we are measured against, however, is based upon a mainstream white female body type. Nonetheless *all* women in this culture suffer from the "not good enough" syndrome when it comes to our bodies. We are compelled to live up to media images that create a body ideal and then program us to strive to attain it. The booming business in diet pills, quick-weight-loss programs, cellulite cream, and in-home exercise gizmos promising instant results demonstrates our obsession with "fixing" our bodies.

The subtle messages we receive seem to say that the only totally acceptable female body type is one that has perfect boobs, a small waist, slim thighs, and a flat stomach. Even women such as the supermodels, whom we perceive as having perfect bodies, become ensnared in this trap. They become obsessed with keeping their bodies perfect lest they be "kicked to the curb" in the modeling industry. From the magazine articles I've read and the "up-close and personal" TV interviews I've seen on supermodels, they also struggle with fully accepting their bodies, since their careers revolve around maintaining the "perfect body." Gaining a few pounds (God forbid!) or having a wrinkle can send a supermodel's self-image and income plunging. And we thought that slim hips and a flat stomach were the answer! The answer lies in fully accepting your body *as it is.* Not after losing a few pounds or getting rid of the cellulite, but right *now.*

Anchored deep in our psyches is pain from the deep-seated

belief that our bodies are not okay, that our bodies are unacceptable. I believe this is why conventional diets and weight-loss programs are ineffective or only temporarily effective—because they don't address this underlying belief that is running us. They try to operate *on top of* our pain instead of first addressing and healing the pain. This keeps us stuck in the pain instead of freeing us to move and go forward.

Healing = Releasing + Forgiveness

This formula applies to all areas of our lives, especially our relationships. And this includes the relationship with our bodies. Healing is what returns us to wholeness.

Sacred Pampering Principle for the Body #2— Making Peace with Your Body

To move from where we are to a place of full body acceptance, we need to make peace with our bodies—the first step toward full bodily self-acceptance. Many of us are at war with our bodies. At an intellectual level we know that we *should* love our bodies. We know we *should* treat them better. We know we *should* embrace them and accept them as they are. But in actuality we don't.

For me, graduating from high school signaled the end of a twelve-year era of year-round sports. In college I gained my "freshman fifteen" and never lost it. Since I had been an athlete from age six to seventeen, my weight had never been an issue. Well, this all changed once I went off to college. This ushered in a new era— one of weight gain and being overly self-conscious about my body.

From my freshman year of college up until about three years ago, weight was a central issue in my life. My college weight gain was primarily the result of eating a lot of the wrong foods, namely high-fat, high-sugar, high-salt foods at the wrong times. Deciding what to wear day to day or to a special event was a big deal. I wore a lot of oversized shirts and sweaters, or jackets long enough to cover my hips. Black stretch pants and stirrup pants were a staple in my wardrobe. And wearing my shirt tucked in where my butt and hips were exposed was definitely a no-no. But once I graduated from college, the issue with my weight shifted from being primarily physical—poor eating habits and lack of adequate exercise—to being more mental, emotional, and psychological. I gained an additional thirty pounds within a couple of years of graduating from college.

For several years I tried, *unsuccessfully,* to permanently lose the forty-five pounds of weight I had gained since graduating from high school. It was both a constant struggle and a constant obsession. I always seemed to be focused on what I was or wasn't eating, how much I was or wasn't exercising, or how well I did or didn't look in my clothes! Several years and many futile attempts later, I decided to stop, take a step back, and ask myself, *Why am I making this so hard?* Something had to be missing. I realized, after some soul-searching, that the struggle and effort to release my excess weight came from operating on top of remnants of pain and anger from my past. I was *mad* at my body.

This realization hit me like a ton of bricks. In that moment I abandoned the incessant search outside of myself for the ideal diet program or exercise videotape or home exercise equipment that would be "the answer" to my weight challenge. I decided to turn inward for the answer. This was a place I hadn't turned to before. I had some healing to do. Over the past six years I've worked to release the core issues underlying my post–high school weight. As part of my healing work I came to realize that my weight continued to be an issue even after college for a different set of reasons: There were areas in my life where I was "weight-ing."

As Black women weight has collectively been a major challenge for us. That's why I think it is particularly useful for us to examine this weight issue within a new context, away from explanations that tend to point to nutrition and exercise exclusively. Through my personal journey with my weight release and listening to testimonies from women in my seminars and workshops, I've found that our weight can represent several kinds of issues. Weight can act as a form of insulation, literally and symbolically. Your weight may be insulating you from fully living, from being able to do what you truly want to do, and from moving about with more ease. Your weight may be insulating you from the pain of not living joyfully and passionately. Or it may be an excuse for not _____ (you fill in the blank). You may be "weighted" down with excuses about why you are not pursuing your dreams and goals, or weighted down with fear of rejection or doubt about your own talents and abilities. It may be insulating you from being touched, receiving sexual attention, or being pampered. It may represent that you are overnurturing others while ignoring your own needs, or that you are weighted down with too much responsibility.

Really give this some *deep* thought, especially if you are personally faced with a weight challenge. Go back to your childhood if you have to. See if you can narrow it down to the specific year when your weight started to become a challenge. Notice what other events, experiences, and dynamics were also going on in your life around that same time. Often weight becomes an issue after a major life change, transition, or traumatic situation, including negative sexual experiences. What do you come up with? Herein lies the key to beginning to unlock and decode this challenge and releasing its grip on you.

In the December 1995 issue of *Essence* magazine I read an article that described this not so uncommon "weighting" phenomenon in an article highlighting the upcoming movie *Waiting to Exhale*. The article describes the four Black female characters as "Women who are waiting to get their careers together. Waiting for the weight to disappear from their hips. Waiting for their children to grow up. But mostly waiting for the men who will finally take their breath away." So what are *you* "weighting" for? Where are you delaying, procrastinating, or holding back? Once you are in touch with the underlying issue(s) at the core of your weight challenge, you can begin to make the internal shift. An internal shift always precedes an external shift.

I was able to release my weight because I finally made the decision to stop *waiting* for opportunities to come my way and started creating them. I started trusting my intuition and abilities and stopped waiting for a "sign-off" or vote of confidence from others before I made bold moves; I stopped waiting for the net to appear before I leaped, and started leaping out on faith with a knowing that the net would appear. And it kept appearing, time after time! I stopped waiting to be validated by a master's or doctorate degree before starting my training and consulting firm; I stopped waiting for men to pamper and nurture me and started pampering and nurturing myself; I stopped waiting for the risk to disappear and started taking action *in spite* of the risk. As I stopped the "weighting," I started gradually releasing the weight.

Beginning the Healing

The next step in my personal healing process was to create loving statements of appreciation for each of the unembraced parts of my body. Before writing down my affirmations I reflected on all of the good and positive associations I could think of for each. For example, instead of looking down at my size ten feet and seeing ugly, flat feet with "corny" toes, I saw a beautiful pair of feet that had taken me many miles in life without fail.

As a little girl these feet had taken me roller skating, playing hopscotch, running, swimming, bicycle riding, and back and forth to school. As a young woman they had taken me to job interviews, victories on the track field, the soccer field, the softball field, the basketball court, and the volleyball court, as well as across a stage to receive a high school diploma and later a college degree. As a grown woman these same feet had taken me down the wedding aisle, to Egypt, up and down sandy beaches in the Caribbean, and up to the podium for my very first speaking engagement.

As I pondered all of the glorious places my feet had taken me, I was reminded of a little story about a man who agonized over having no shoes. This man was very anxious and worried about which shoes to buy, until he met a man who had no feet. I needed to be thankful that I even *have* feet. There are those who are born without feet or have lost a foot in an accident. And all I could think about was their *perceived* imperfections. Focusing on imperfections *definitely* does not lead to peace of mind and unconditional acceptance. The key was accepting my feet *in spite of* their imperfections.

Next I created some loving statements of appreciation for my feet. I sat down and decided to take a really *good* look at them. The more closely I looked, the more I realized that they really had some very redeeming qualities. Some of the affirmations I created for my feet were: "Thank you for having ten toes. Thank you for keeping me balanced. Thank you for keeping me grounded. Thank you for continuing to hold my body up every day. Thank you for taking me all the places that I've wanted you to go." In addition to saying these statements to my feet, I started to spend more time touching and rubbing them instead of condemning them. Gradually my outward behavior toward my feet began to change for the better as my inner thoughts about them started to change for the better. As a result I started taking better care of them and giving them more attention—giving them periodic pedicures, painting my toenails, massaging them.

It is time for us to make peace with our bodies. Here's a poem I was inspired to write about the beauty of fully accepting the body you have:

Wanted

Wanted . . .
Women who flaunt it because they got it.
Who hug their curves
And liberate their swerves
And make no apologies.

Wanted . . .
Women who are comfortable in their skin
And honor their bodies
As Divine Temples of the Creator

Wanted . . .
Women who can lovingly run a hand
Over buxom breast or rounded bottom
And feel no need to minimize their lovely thighs
And know they are worthy of pleasure now, not later.

Wanted . . .
Women whose hips sashay
And love to sway

Even if they bump a table or two
They keep on swayin'
Without delayin'
Because they know there's more bumpin' to do.

Yes, you'll see her comin' with her head held high
And a confident smile parting her lips.
She's been doing her body embracing
And she is no longer at war with her hips.

I can vividly recall a pivotal experience I had while getting a pedicure that I considered confirmation of the positive effects of making peace with my feet. For Mother's Day a few years ago my husband gave me a gift called A Day of Pampering at an upscale full-service beauty salon. My Day of Pampering included a pedicure, facial, lunch, manicure, and makeover. As the day drew nearer, I started to get a little nervous about exposing my feet to a pedicurist who, I was sure, looked at dainty, perfect feet all day long. On the day of my appointment I arrived at the salon and changed into the robe they had for me. The first service I was to receive was my pedicure. I took a seat on the pedicurist's station with a bit of trepidation. As she started to lower my feet into the warm, sudsy water of the vibrating foot bath, she quietly commented, "Nice feet." I almost fell out of the chair. *Did she say, "Nice feet"?* Instantly I had the urge to start proving her wrong by pointing out all my feet's imperfections. But I caught myself. I took a deep breath, smiled graciously, said, "Thank you," and lowered my feet down into the water.

Wow, I thought to myself, *when was the last time someone told me I had nice feet, or ever told me I had nice feet?* After my pedicure was over, I quietly asked the pedicurist, "So what makes my feet so nice?" She replied that my feet were smooth and uncallused and that there was no hardened dead skin or cracking around the edges of the heels.

To anyone else this incident may have seemed insignificant, but for me, given my past relationship with my feet, it was a minor miracle. I knew I'd come a long way with my foot-embracing process. I looked down at my freshly painted toes and replied, "Yes, they *are* nice, aren't they?"

My toes had been a major source of insecurity for me up until just a couple of years ago. I thought they were ugly. A few others did, too, based on their comments. They weren't dainty (I wear a size ten) and perfect like the feet I saw in magazines or TV advertisements. I'd been a year-round athlete from age six up until age seventeen, and in those eleven years my feet and toes had taken a beatin'! Eddie Murphy's character, Marcus, from the movie *Boomerang* would say my toes had had serious "hammertime." As a result I became a master at hiding and covering up my toes. I avoided open-toed shoes. Now, this may sound a little ridiculous to you, but for me it was very real.

A couple of years ago I really got to thinking about this issue I had with my toes. Combined with the other major area of my body where I had an issue—my knock-knees—I realized that it was time to make a shift. I was in bondage. I wasn't free because I was so concerned about being sure to cover up my toes, or to wear shorts and skirts that were long enough to minimize my knock-knees. This compensating and strategizing got to the point where it had become automatic.

Then, after having my second daughter, Kiana, another issue joined the body-issues party—my breasts. I had always been clear about the decision to breast-feed. I'd been given the various tips and techniques to use, suggestions on how to pump, the type of nursing bra to buy—all that. But I wasn't fully aware of how my breasts were going to look after breast-feeding two babies. *They were droopy!* I hadn't planned on droopy breasts as part of the breast-feeding package. So, feeling good about my breasts after breast-feeding two babies was not an easy task.

Even though my husband said they were fine with him, I still kept trippin' for a couple months after my second daughter was weaned. As long as I kept wishing and hoping that my breasts would look different, somehow reinflate or resume their prior perkiness, I was both miserable and insecure about them. It didn't matter what my husband or anyone else thought. What mattered was what *I* thought about my breasts. It took me several more months to grasp the reality that I wasn't less attractive, less feminine, or less of a woman because my boobs drooped. I had to "get" that I was the same woman, with or without saggy boobs! I was able to recover from the "If Only" Syndrome after a conscious process of healing and body-acceptance work.

As I've moved through this process of weight release, self-hugs and written affirmations have played an important part in my journey. Self-hugs allow you to give love energy back to yourself. Stand up right now and give a self-hug a try. Here's how you do my version of a self-hug: Wrap your arms around yourself up near your shoulders. Take a deep breath. Now close your eyes and slightly drop your chin into the hollow created by your crossed arms. Take two deep breaths. On each exhale melt down and let your chin drop farther into your chest. Take two more deep breaths while relaxing your shoulders and body more with each breath. Remain in this position for at least a full minute. Doesn't this feel good?

I also began doing more things for myself that demonstrated that I loved myself. This included building more Quiet Time into my daily life. Integrating pampering and Quiet Time into my life were two changes that made a huge difference. As I started *actively* valuing and loving myself more, my weight slowly but surely began to fall away.

In conjunction with my body-acceptance and weight-release process, I've made some other gradual adjustments in my life over the past several years. I've increased my awareness of what does and does not serve my body temple's highest good. I've virtually eliminated carbonated drinks, red meat, pork, and fried foods from my eating choices. I've started drinking more water and more herbal tea, and snacking less. If I decide, once in a while, to make the *conscious* choice to have some ice cream or some barbecued ribs, I let it be okay—no guilt trips. These gradual shifts have been baby steps, but nonetheless they've been forward motion. Most important, I'm happy and satisfied because I am making gradual and *permanent* progress. Even an inch forward is an inch better.

When actress Lynn Whitfield gave the closing keynote address at the African-American Women on Tour conference in Atlanta, Georgia, in August 1995, she made a point that still sticks out in my mind. In her speech she challenged us to move through life periodically asking ourselves, *Is this serving me?* She related this question to our bodies, and most specifically to what we put in our bodies and subject them to. She said that whether you're smoking, drinking, getting high, or about to eat a second bowlful of fudge ice cream, the question to ask yourself is, *Is this serving me?* "If the answer is no," she said with an intense, sweeping glance of the audience, *"then stop it."* Later I revisited this question in my mind, and it got me thinking: *What is it that keeps me doing things to my body that I know don't serve it?* I know what to do, but why don't I do what I *know?* I concluded that what these situations revealed is where I had more body embracing and healing work to do.

Body Embracing

A powerful part of the journey to fuller body acceptance is *touching* your body more—focusing on the more "unembraced" parts. Notice how we tend *not* to touch the areas of our bodies we have a hard time fully embracing? A loving touch does wonders for the body. What do you need to touch more? Is it those "too wide" hips, that "too big" butt, that "too broad" nose, or that "too short" hair?

It is best to practice this body-embracing touching when you are naked so that you can see yourself in full view. A good time is in the morning before you get dressed, in the evenings before you get into bed, or after your bath or shower. Focus on one area of your body per week. Stand in front of a large mirror, full-length preferably, and take three minutes to slowly look yourself over from head to toe. Take in the shapes and distinct curves that are part of you. To work on body embracing with your thighs, for example, you might want to rub some body oil into your hands and then, one thigh at a time, slowly and gently glide both hands up, down, and around. Take your time. Send your thighs loving thoughts as you embrace them.

You may want to make up a set of affirmations for yourself on colored three-by-five-inch index cards. I made a complete set of these homemade affirmation cards that helped me to address my body-temple issues as well as other areas of holistic personal growth such as: healing and forgiveness, prosperity, positive relationships, personal power, pampering, self-nurturing, communications, and the Goddess principles. As part of my embracing process I took the cards and taped them up around my house, in my bathroom and in my bedroom, and I even put a few in my daily planner. I wanted to be reminded to affirm myself every day. At my previous home I had affirmations plastered all over one wall in the bathroom. People would go in to use the bathroom and would come out inspired!

The affirmation cards were so effective and useful for me that I had some professionally produced and started making them available in my seminars and workshops for purchase. If you're not up to making your own set of affirmation cards, you can order personal sets from the order form in the back of the book.

My faith in myself has deepened and grown, as well as my understanding of how my faith shows up in my actions. I am no longer at war with my body, but am now well on my way to a lasting peace. As I've continued the process of releasing and forgiving, I've noticed how my body is becoming a spiritual ally and friend, instead of a disconnected, nonspiritual system of flesh, blood, and organs.

My most profound realization is that the process of healing and embracing my body has also been a process of *revaluing* my body as a temple. The key to changing my relationship to my body was first revaluing it. I had to recognize its sacred value before I could give it greater respect and, in turn, actively demonstrate love of it. My concept of self-love is now expanded far beyond the single dimension represented by self-confidence to being a holistic, multidimensional expression that describes holding my mind, spirit, *and* body in high esteem.

SACRED PAMPERING PRINCIPLE FOR THE BODY #3— CREATING SACRED SPACES AND PLACES

To counter the erosive affects of contemporary living, we need special spaces to take our bodies to where we can relax, nurture, and love them. We need these special spaces and places so that we can seek refuge from the onslaught of modern living. Sacred spaces and places are those that are "dedicated to or set apart for a purpose."

When I was a little girl, I remember our living room and also my parents' bedroom being these types of places. The living room was off-limits. My sister and I were not allowed to take shortcuts through the living room to get to our bedroom. We had to go the long way, down the hallway. Mama made it clear that the living room was reserved for company and special holiday gatherings, such as Christmas or Kwanzaa. At that tender, young age I didn't realize that she wanted us to recognize the living room as a sacred place—a place with a special purpose.

It was much the same with my parents' bedroom. The only time I was allowed to enter it without permission was when I was putting away laundry for Mama or Daddy or getting my hair combed before church on Sunday morning. To me their room was like a sanctuary. I would never think of jumping on their bed or shouting while I was in their bedroom. My parents' bedroom was a sacred place.

As a little girl I had a special reverence for our living room and my parents' bedroom because of the reverence created around them. In much the same way, we need to create sanctity around places in our lives. Spaces and places we give special meaning to serve a special purpose. They allow us to enjoy solitude, gather our thoughts without interruption, get grounded, connect with the Creator, connect with ourselves, or connect with others. Having sacred places helps to ground and center us in the midst of a potentially overwhelming world.

As descendants of ancient indigenous people, Black folks have a legacy founded on honoring sacred places in our lives. But I think many of us feel scattered and spiritually disconnected because we don't have places to retreat to in order to get refocused and grounded. This is why sacred places and spaces are so important.

My bedroom is one of my special spaces. I consider it to be my and my husband's sanctuary. It is our haven, our refuge. And I've arranged it to reflect this. I've chosen soothing colors and a furniture arrangement that shows that it is more than just a place for sleeping at night. We have a lamp that sits on a nightstand beside our bed for gentler lighting. We have plenty of pillows for back-propping, and I have a chintz backrest for writing or reading in bed. We have a wooden ceiling fan to keep air circulating freely. Lovely pictures hang on the walls. We listen to relaxing jazz and classical music on a compact disc/audiocassette player. I also keep plenty of candles and incense on hand in our bedroom. To seal in the good energy, we keep our bedroom door closed during the day so that others know it's off-limits. Family members included. They know to ask permission if they need to enter our room.

*   *   *

Think about what sacred places and spaces you can create in or around your home. If you can designate a sacred place that is outdoors in nature, too, even better. One of my sisterfriends has a special tree she goes to for her spiritual time. In the summertime there are two little parks I like to go to near my home, especially for journaling, relaxing, or goal setting. Being next to the trees, the birds, and the grass is soothing to my soul. Seek out at least two places or spaces you can designate as your sanctuary or special refuge. Your special place may be under a tree, on your patio, in your bathroom, a special spot by a lake, or a corner in the garden.

SACRED PAMPERING PRINCIPLE FOR THE BODY #4— CREATING RITUALS

An important part of the path to self-care for us African Americans is to return to rituals as a means of reconnecting with ourselves and our greatness within. A ritual is an action or activity that has a greater symbolic or spiritual meaning. Ritual is powerful because it takes you beyond the visible, the rational, and the obvious to grasp larger and deeper meanings. This is why those who participate in a ritual together feel closer and more bonded afterward. Malidoma Some, in *Ritual: Power, Healing & Community*, says this: "I am tempted to think that when the focus of everyday living displaces ritual in a given society, social decay begins to work from the inside out. The fading and disappearance of ritual in modern culture is . . . the weakening of links with the spirit world, and general alienation of people from themselves and others."

Our personal rituals can range from the simple to the complex. Rituals are distinct from traditions or routines, however. Traditions do not necessarily have spiritual components and are usually centered around holidays in the American culture. The same applies to routines. Routines can be habitual, such as the sequence you follow when getting ready for work in the morning. Routines, however, do not have symbolic or spiritual meaning. They're usually functional. Rituals are spiritual processes created to achieve specific outcomes. And the process is as valuable and significant as the outcome itself. With a ritual, you cannot separate the journey from the outcome; they are intrinsically intertwined. Rituals generate closeness and can give extra-ordinary meaning to events, experiences, and group gatherings. They actually *invoke* emotions that foster bonding and intimacy.

Saying grace before a meal is a food-blessing ritual. Baptism is a religious ritual that represents a rebirth, or being "born again." Marriage is a spiritual ritual that represents the joining of two spirits as well as the initiation into a divine relationship.

When performing a ritual, you should use a ritual object. A ritual object serves as a symbol that can help evoke meaning, feelings, and emotions. It can also help us connect with the spiritual realm and invoke personal change at a far greater speed and at a deeper level than is possible through language and words alone. For example in certain Native American cultures, the "talking stick" is a ritual object. Whoever holds the talking stick in the sacred circle has the privilege of speaking without interruption, while others listen fully and respectfully.

Your personal pampering ritual objects may be a certain candle, a piece of African fabric, or even a rock. Your ritual objects have special meaning for you. And in turn they should be treated with care and respect. The ritual objects you select should strike a resonant chord in you. For example you may select a certain rock that to you represents Mother Earth. Or you may choose a certain candle because it represents the Light of Love that dwells within you. The symbolic objects you choose to use in your rituals are powerful because of the meaning *you* associate them with. Other ritual objects may be a piece of jewelry, a photograph, a plant, a crystal, an angel figurine, a leaf, a pressed flower, a piece of African fabric, or a cowrie shell.

Another important part of the framework for a ritual is Sacred Ritual Time. Sacred Ritual Time is special time set aside for your ritual. Sacred Ritual Time means ensuring that you won't be interrupted—by ringing telephones, radio, TV, friends, spouse, or your children. Set yourself up to *win*. As preparation for your ritual ask yourself, *Is there anything to keep me from focusing and devoting my attention and focus to my ritual?* If so, handle it in advance.

An Altar—Your Personal Worship Center

In my bedroom I have a small altar. My altar serves as a personal spiritual center for my prayer, meditation, and reflection. Don't let the word *altar* intimidate or confuse you; it has many connotations and may conjure up images from your religious upbringing. A personal altar is a sacred place for focusing your spiritual energy and practices. Just as you might go to the health club to work out or to your kitchen to cook a meal, your altar is a place to go to for your personal spiritual activities.

My altar is a small white two-level shelf. On it are keepsakes, special mementos, and symbolic objects in addition to candles, poetry, inspirational quotes, a book of daily affirmations, an album with special thank-you letters and cards of love and support from my Sistercircle, and my "Wish Box," a cloth-covered, lidded box in which I keep my three-month goals, and my most special cards and letters.

Each object on my altar has special meaning. For example I have things such as a picture of my parents, a picture of me and my husband, a set of altar cards, a special set of cards with spiritual truths and affirmations written on them that I use during my prayer and meditation time, a little black terra-cotta angel given to me by one of my sisterfriends, the handmade African-fabric handkerchiefs that we give out as keepsakes at the annual Black women's gathering that I conceived, a friendship poem, two jumbo quartz crystals, a glass heart, several pieces of red rock and alabaster I gathered when I was in Luxor and Aswan, Egypt, in the summer of 1992, and miniature seashells from my trip to the Caribbean. I also keep a colorful supply of candles and an assortment of incense there.

On your altar you may decide to have a blue candle, a symbol of peace and serenity; a small plant to represent nature, abundance, and growth; a flower to represent beauty; a piece of African fabric to remind you of your heritage and your connection to the Motherland; a picture of Harriet Tubman to represent the warrior woman spirit; and a photo of your family to represent your legacy.

With regard to your candleholders, and other objects on your altar especially, use silver whenever possible. Silver attracts and amplifies the power of the moon, which represents the feminine, Goddess energy. If silver is too difficult for you to obtain, use crystal or glass.

Erecting my altar had a snowball effect. I initiated a little "altar movement" among my circle of close sisterfriends. So now each of us has an altar that reflects our individual personalities and styles. A personal altar should be a reflection of you. You may decide to create a marriage altar or a family altar as well. Community altars play an important part in community Kwanzaa celebrations, for example.

When I am sitting at my altar, I like to light a candle and begin with a couple of deep, cleansing breaths. Occasionally I'll burn some incense during my altar time. I usually start with a prayer of thanks for the blessings the Creator has allowed me throughout the day. In preparation for my next day, especially if I have a presentation, speaking engagement, or client training, I'll create an inner image of how I'd like my day to go and flow. If I have any concerns I need to release, or if I need to forgive someone, I do that, too, during my altar time.

I usually complete my altar time by reading an affirmation or inspirational poem from the small collection of daily affirmation books that sit on the bottom shelf of my altar. Sometimes I choose to close by reading one of my altar cards and meditating on its message. (See the order form in the back of this book for a listing of items you might like to order.)

To grow spiritually and deepen my personal relationships, I've started incorporating rituals as a regular part of my life. For example I've created a friendship ritual that I practice regularly now that I have more flexibility and control over my time. At least twice a month I arrange to have tea with a friend, either at my home or at the Wellington, a local, Black-owned Victorian tearoom. I especially try to arrange tea time with friends whom I don't get to see often or who have extremely hectic schedules. This tea-sharing ritual is a chance to enjoy some cozy conversation in a peaceful, unrushed setting. If the tea-sharing ritual takes place at my home, I have special cups and saucers in which I serve a special selection of herbal teas. If the tea-sharing rituals takes place at the Wellington, we share a special pot of the Republic of Tea's Ginger-Peach tea.

Then there is the Empowerment Party ritual, which is done with a group of your closest sisterfriends and was begun by my sisterfriend Alma Lorraine in January 1995. The Empowerment Party ritual is a way for us to help each other launch a new phase in our lives, mark a turning point, or celebrate a triumph, in the form of an overnight slumber-party-style gathering.

Alma Lorraine decided that she wanted to start her new year off with a focus on her health and wellness. So that became the theme of her Empowerment Party. She asked one of her sisterfriends to be her hostess and coordinator, gave an invitation list to her, and asked her to invite those of us on the guest list to share in this special overnight gathering. Alma Lorraine's purpose for having the Empowerment Party was to create an evening surrounded by loving sisterfriends where she would receive the support and encouragement she needed for this new phase of her life focusing on her health and wellness. She wanted it to be an evening of celebration and joy.

Her Empowerment Party hostess sent out beautiful, elegant invitations with specific instructions that we were to follow as the special guests. It instructed us to bring a healthy homemade food dish, a theme-related gift, and a letter of support for Alma Lorraine's Health and Wellness Support Album. And of course a sleeping bag for staying overnight, personal items, and a bathing suit for the late-night rap session in Alma Lorraine's hot tub.

When I arrived at Alma Lorraine's, her hostess escorted me to the den to join her other sisterfriends in a homecooked potluck feast served by candlelight. We ate off of fine china, drank out of crystal wineglasses, and laughed, talked, and bonded, while the sexy, soothing voice of Luther Vandross crooned from the stereo. It was much like the well-known birthday scene out of the movie *Waiting to Exhale.* It was a night to remember. After dinner we took places on the floor in a circle and came forward one by one to present Alma Lorraine with our gifts and letters of support. After receiving our gifts and letters she shared her health and wellness goals with us. She had established a specific weight-release and exercise plan for herself that she shared, asking for our support and encouragement along the way.

This party was such a deeply touching and enjoyable experience that at the end I asked Alma Lorraine for permission to re-create the event based upon her model. Of course she agreed. Hence the Empowerment Party ritual was born.

A couple of months later I decided to have a Prosperity Party in celebration of the tremendous success of "For Sisters Only: Sharing, Healing, and Renewal," the First Annual Pacific Northwest African-American Women's Advance, which I founded. To me prosperity represented health, wealth, and abundance, and I decided that what was next for me was having health, wealth, and happiness reflected in all areas of my life.

Over the next twelve months several other friends had Empowerment Parties, patterning our individual parties after the model established by Alma Lorraine. Our various Empowerment Party themes have included: Focus, Love Relationships, Divine Mate, Self-love, and Spiritual Obedience. These Empowerment Parties have definitely added a new dimension of depth and bonding to our sisterfriendships. The beauty of this and other rituals is that they are unique, participative experiences. They are not meant to be explained or described to someone who wasn't there—they are meant to be experienced.

Having two little children has taught us that one-on-one time together is precious. So my husband and I consistently carve out time just for the two of us. One way we do this is with a morning reading ritual. Twice a month we get up before the girls awaken and enjoy quiet reading time together in the living room. Part of our ritual is sipping from cups of hot apple cider or Ginger Peach tea while we sit quietly on the couch listening to soft jazz while my husband reads his morning paper and I read a book.

Using ritual, I added a new dimension to our family Thanksgiving Day gatherings. I created a Gratitude Ritual. For as far back as I can remember, at each Thanksgiving Day meal our family would hold hands, my dad would say grace to bless the food, then we would indulge in a host of delicious dishes Mama had prepared. Eating was definitely the focus of our Thanksgivings. So several years ago I thought it would be nice to add a new dimension to our Thanksgiving Day that would put more emphasis on giving thanks. I asked my parents for their permission to introduce a simple predinner ritual and they complied.

The Gratitude Ritual required that we dim the lights and all stand up around the table holding hands. I lit a white candle and placed it in a candleholder. The candle is passed around one by one so that each person has an opportunity to reflect on his or her year and to share what he or she is most thankful for. During these sacred moments you can feel the love fill the room as friends and family members share from their hearts, expressing thanks for health, provision, faith, strength, safety, an accomplishment, the love for a spouse, or family unity. I've watched family and friends participate in this ritual over the past several years, and it is touching to hear them share thanks from their hearts as the candle is passed to them. It is not unusual to see eyes brimming or a tear fall down a cheek. After this ritual I feel like I have a deeper gratitude for the family and friends who are gathered and also for the blessings in my life.

Even in writing this book I created a writing ritual so that it would not feel like a laborious task but instead would be a joy. I decided to write the initial manuscript draft in longhand in unlined journals instead of going the high-tech route of typing it directly into my computer. It may have taken me longer to do a longhand version first instead of typing it directly into the computer, but this is what worked for me. I created a writing ritual in which I would prepare a cup of herbal tea, retreat into my office, put on my high-toned, relaxing music, select two of my special writing pens from my pen collection, settle into the chair at my wide draftsperson's-style desk, and have a writing session. Although I had a manuscript deadline to meet, writing this book continued to be an absolute joy, through to the end. The ritual gave my book-writing process new meaning and reframed it into a larger experience, an experience in which I was "midwifing" something into the world that had potential to transform women's lives, those of their families, and in turn their communities and even their workplaces.

In what areas of your life would rituals make a difference? Do you have a task or activity that has become mundane and needs some spicing up? A relationship that's lost its luster? A friendship that's gotten distant? Want to increase the bonding and intimacy between you and a lover, husband, or other family member? Create a ritual.

A couple of months before my first daughter, Adera, was born, I wanted to make the African proverb, "It takes a whole village to raise a child," a reality. Baby showers traditionally are for women only, and I wanted to create a special event that would allow men and children to participate as well. So I created an event called a Welcome to the World Party, which would take place *after* Adera was born so that she could be there too. Family and close friends were invited to this potluck-style celebration. The age of our guests ranged from five months to fifty years, and everyone came together to share good food, laughter, love, and the celebration of a new life coming into the world. It was a beautiful afternoon.

Before the celebration came to a close, we called everyone together in the living room to join hands in a circle for a "village ritual." Joe and I acknowledged those in the circle as our village and explained what their love and support was going to mean to us as new parents. We gave others a chance to share words of wisdom and encouragement with us, then closed with a prayer led by the proud grandparents. The Welcome to the World Party we had for Adera was such a success that I decided to do it again several months later after the birth of my sister's baby, Kalii.

Follow your heart and intuition when it comes to creating a new ritual. The possibilities are endless. When I know a ritual is needed for an event or an experience but am not clear about the how and what of it, I pray about it, asking for the appropriate ritual to be revealed to me. The answer always comes.

Sacred Pampering Principle for the Body #5— Creating an In-Home Spa

Many of us have an untapped pampering resource in our homes that we are not fully utilizing—our bathtubs! We've gotten used to taking showers instead of baths because showers are quicker. In the time that it takes for our bathwater to run, we could be in and out of the shower and even dried off. As our society continues to find ways to do things quicker and faster, relaxation rituals are getting squeezed out. In taking a look back through the ages, however, we see that bathing has historically served a dual purpose—for cleanliness and as therapy. We are going to take a look at the latter, at bathing as a therapeutic process, as a ritual of relaxation.

In ancient Egypt, for example, our African ancestors bathed in the mighty Nile River for purposes of removing negative energy and renewing the spirit. In third-century Rome the baths were social centers where men and women could be steamed, bathed, oiled, and rubbed down. The bathing ritual, which reached its height in the early second century A.D., could take as long as five hours! This practice began to disappear with the decline of the Roman Empire when the Roman perception of bathing changed as strict religious church policies were imposed. The perception of bathing changed from one of being honorable and dignified to one of being sinful and decadent.

Bathing for therapeutic purposes is a lost art that needs to be fully revived. If we look back to the early indigenous cultures that shaped human civilization, we see many mystical and spiritual attributes ascribed to water. Bathing was highly regarded in these cultures because water was believed to have divine powers. An ancient Arab proverb says, "Water is the most healing of all remedies and the best of all cosmetics." To treat water carelessly was to invite the wrath of the spirits and the condemnation of the community. Societies such as the Australian Aborigines believed their water holes to be sacred.

Many bathing customs are revealed in the sacred writings of India, Africa, and the Middle East. Water purification ceremonies are depicted in the temples of ancient Egypt, and described in the Old Testament and the Koran. Faithful Mohammedans still observe the washing ritual before prayer. Baptism by water is a sacrament in many of the world's religions. It has its roots among the societies that lived in the ancient Nile Valley. The Nile River was sacred to the Egyptians, and the Ganges River to the Hindus. And the fifteenth-century knights were ceremoniously bathed before being dubbed, not for cleanliness of the body but for purity of the spirit.

Bathing plays an important part in my personal pampering rituals. I remember how Mama was always partial to baths over showers. For me she elevated bathing to an art. She called her hour-long bath a soak. As a little girl I didn't understand why taking a bath was such a big deal. To me taking a bath was for getting the dirt off. Now I understand how important Mama's soaks were for pampering her body, clearing her mind, and renewing her spirit.

To understand the full impact of bathing, it is useful to be aware of some of the spiritual properties of water. Water plays a key role in our physical birthing process. We are suspended in a water-filled environment for nine months while we are in the womb. Water is a recurring theme around issues of cleansing, purging, renewal, and rebirth. The surface of Mother Earth is 75 percent water, our bodies are 75 percent water, and water constitutes 99 percent of the molecules that make up our bodies.

Water also has fascinating chemical properties. It has the unique ability to absorb and hold subtle energy. Your body has a subtle energy field that is electromagnetic and surrounds it, responding to the electromagnetic charge of your various emotions. Another word for this external subtle energy field is *aura*. The water in your bath can act like a sponge and literally absorb negative energy. This is why after a bath you feel not only cleaner but refreshed.

A pampering bath is a ritual unto itself that can be done in the privacy of your own home. By definition a spa is a resort having mineral springs. So it requires that we use a little imagination and some bath additives to turn our bathroom and bathtub into an in-home spa. Twice a month I schedule pampering baths. I set aside at least an hour to indulge, without interruption. With my pampering baths I give myself ten minutes just for preparation so that I can lay out my assortment of pampering tools and supplies.

Essential oils are an integral part of my pampering baths. Each essential oil has a different "tone," just like notes on a piano. Knowing the tone, or properties, of an essential oil can help you know how to use them properly for therapeutic purposes in your bath. Essential oils can help you anchor or change a mood or emotion. Depending on the mood you're in, the different properties of essential oils can evoke different effects. Here's some introductory information on the properties of some of the more popular essential oils since they are great for adding to your bathwater. You only need two to three drops *per tubful* if you are using pure essential oils.

Essential Oil	*Properties*
Chamomile	Calming and soothing
Citronella	Purifying and deodorizing
Eucalyptus	Energy balancing
Frankincense	Revitalizing
Grapefruit	Energizing and uplifting
Jasmine	Soothing and healing
Lavender	Healing and calming
Myrrh	Revitalizing, fortifying

Essential Oil	*Properties*
Neroli	Stimulating to the heart chakra
Orange	Energizing and uplifting
Rose	Uplifting and regenerating
Sandalwood	Elevating and opening
Tangerine	Energizing and uplifting
Ylang-ylang	Stimulating and euphoric, aphrodisiac

Let's say you've had a crazy, want-to-pull-your-hair-out kind of day. Add a few drops of chamomile or jasmine essential oil to your bathwater to calm and soothe you. Feeling a little low or sad? Add some grapefruit, orange, tangerine, or frankincense oil to your bathwater to lift your spirits. Feeling aroused, especially sensual, or in the mood for love? Add some neroli or ylang-ylang. If you want to affect your mood without taking a pampering bath, try a diffuser. Or, for a homespun alternative, put a small pot of water on the stove on medium high. Put a few drops of essential oil in the water once it starts to steam and the scent will gently fill the air.

Bathing's Health Benefits

Did you know that bathing also has health benefits? In addition to serving an important therapeutic and spiritual purpose, bathing also has an important biological purpose. The skin, which is the largest organ of the body, serves four basic functions: sensory, excretory, heat regulating, and respiratory. The latter two functions are most affected by bathing.

Our skin is made up of several complex layers, with the topmost layer containing melanin, the protein substance that gives our skin its rich coloring. The entire surface of our skin is shed every twenty-eight days and is replaced by new healthy tissue. Bathing helps to remove old, dead skin so that your sebaceous and sweat glands don't get clogged. Your sebaceous glands secrete sebum, the fatty substance that keeps your skin pliable and lubricated. Bathing is also important to peripheral circulation in those tiny veins and capillaries close to the surface of the skin. Using a body loofah or body brush helps remove the dead skin. Water cleanses, detoxifies, and deodorizes your skin and helps it to remain healthy, elastic, and supple.

SACRED PAMPERING PRINCIPLE FOR THE BODY #6— FREEING YOUR SELF OF DIS-EASE

Health, which is defined as a state of wholeness and balance, does not only pertain to our physical selves, as we've been conditioned to believe by conventional medicine. It relates to our tridimensional selves—mind, body, and spirit. Health, then becomes an interrelated web of physical, mental, emotional, and spiritual dynamics that affect one another. But in order to achieve tridimensional fitness, we must be very clear about how our bodies respond to and manifest *dis-ease.*

Let's first look a little closer at the word *dis-ease. Ease,* according to Webster's Dictionary is "freedom from worry, pain, or agitation." *Dis* is a prefix that negates the word it precedes. It converts a word to its opposite (e.g., *disarray, disengage, disappear, disconnect*). So dis-ease in our minds, bodies, or spirits is an unnatural, agitated, out-of-balance state. In *You Can Heal Your Life,* counselor and metaphysical teacher Louise Hay says, "I believe that we create every so-called 'illness' in our body. The body, like everything else in life, is a mirror of our inner thoughts and beliefs. The body is always talking to us, if we will only take the time to listen." So when your body is in a state of dis-ease, it is sending you some very important messages. I think dis-ease, pain, and illness are our body's way of trying to get our undivided attention.

To have a better understanding of the nature of dis-ease, it is useful to examine and explore the mental, emotional, and spiritual origins that are at the *source* of dis-ease. Before we begin this exploration, there are several myths to bust and crack wide open regarding physical dis-ease. If we hope to truly shift our perspective, we have to bust up the myths that have created the illusions that have been *fueling* our attitudes, thoughts, and beliefs about sickness and illness.

Naturopaths, homeopaths, energy workers, body workers, spiritual healers, and metaphysicians of the nineteenth and twentieth centuries are confirming what our ancient African, East Indian, and other indigenous cultures of color have been accepting as *basic* truths for centuries: *Our bodies respond physically, spiritually, and mentally to our thoughts, emotions, and beliefs.*

Self-care also enables us to take back our power when it comes to healing our bodies. We've relinquished personal power and responsibility for our healing to doctors, surgeons, and medical "experts." Their role should be to *facilitate* the healing of our bodies, not to be the authority over them. They may be experts on our *physical* body, our anatomy and physiology, but they are not experts on our thoughts and emotions, which we now realize play an integral role in our health at the cause level.

Every thought and emotion we experience causes a chemical response in our bloodstream, our organs, and our immune system. Repressed negative emotions trigger dissonant vibrations in the body, which can ultimately lead to dis-ease. Emotions such as anger, frustration, rage, anxiety, and resentment have a lower vibration than positive emotions. Over time negative thoughts, ideas, and emotions can pile up and create kinks and blockages in the normally smooth, continuous flow of the body's *chi energy*. The areas in our bodies that are the site of these pile-ups and blockages of negative energy become weakened and vulnerable to dis-ease. *Chi* is an ancient Chinese word used to describe the body's vital life force. It is this same chi energy that flows through the chakras, the body's primary centers of energy. If the negative mental and emotional states contributing to the kinks and blockages persist, physical dis-ease eventually manifests in the physical body.

Within the last decade there have been significant increases in specific types of physical dis-ease among women in general, and Black women in particular. This rise in certain types of dis-eases indicates a major crisis. Black women are disproportionately manifesting dis-eases that are anchored in the feminine and reproductive organs—*the breasts, uterus, ovaries, vagina, and cervix.* What this tells me, in bright, bold, *screaming* neon letters, is that we are literally dying from lack of being nurtured, lack of self-nurturing, and repression of our feminine energies. We also need to know that *dis-ease that locates in our feminine organs is often caused by unresolved bitterness, anger, and resentment toward men*—usually a father, father figure, close male relative, or (ex-) husband. Severe menstrual cramps are also a sign of rejection of the feminine principle and an imbalance of the male and female energies.

The number one physical dis-ease that results from unexpressed, unreleased, repressed anger and resentment is *cancer.* Among Black women, in this last decade especially, there has been a meteoric rise in breast cancer, cancer of the cervix and the uterus, and cysts and fibroids on the uterine wall or ovaries. If cancer is a manifestation of festering anger and harboring resentments, the first question to ask is, *Anger and resentment at whom and about what?* The anger and resentment that is manifesting as cancer in our female organs is connected to: unresolved issues from past relationships; anger and bitterness toward your father (whether present or absent from the home); unhealed emotional pain from molestation, rape, or sexual abuse; compounded disappointment and frustration from a current or past marriage; or lack of touching, bonding, intimacy, or orgasms.

Louise Hay, a spiritual counselor who healed herself of cancer, explains in her book, *You Can Heal Your Life,* that the mental and emotional *root cause* of cancer is a "deep resentment held for a long time until it literally eats away at the body. Deep secrets or grief eating away at the self. Carrying hatreds." Another pattern she noticed among people with cancer is that they were individuals who "lived with a sense of self-pity, finding it hard to develop and maintain long-term, meaningful relationships." In the back of Hay's book she provides an alphabetical listing of bodily dis-eases, an explanation of the mental or emotional probable causes, and affirmations to provide new thought patterns for reversing the dis-ease.

When the normally smooth flow of energy through the body

starts to kink up, it weakens the area around the kink. It's usually in these weakened, vulnerable areas that dis-ease manifests. It becomes clear that there are many kinks and blockages in the psyches of Black women around men-related anger and resentment. It is time for us to release ourselves from this bondage and to heal.

I consult Louise Hay's book whenever I feel the slightest early symptoms of sickness coming on or any physical discomfort. I try to derail and dismantle the toxic mental and emotional thoughts before they flourish into full-fledged sickness. I even have family and friends call me up to find out what "the book" says about the root cause of a sickness they may be experiencing.

The power of self-healing as a result of identifying and decoding underlying mental and emotional causes is a phenomenon I've witnessed in my own life as well as in that of others I've encountered in seminars and retreats. A personal experience that occurred in June 1995 comes to mind, one that underscores the profound relationship that exists between the mind and the body. It happened shortly after I had submitted the final version of my book proposal to my literary agent after a seven-month process of drafts, rewrites, and edits. On this particular June morning I got out of bed to begin my day, but after being up for about an hour I decided to lie back down for a quick catnap while my husband and daughters ate breakfast. As I arose from my ten-minute nap, my neck froze up and a sharp pain shot up my neck and into my scalp. I thought to myself, *What the hell is going on?* My neck had been perfectly fine just ten minutes before. I hadn't gotten up abruptly or been lying down with my neck in a weird position. I rose slowly and sat up dumbfounded. I tried to turn my head slightly to the right and then to the left. When I turned my head slightly either way, the searing pain shot up my neck and into my scalp. Placing my hands on either side of my neck as a sort of brace, I managed to stand up and slowly move down the hall to the dining room where my family was sitting. Standing there in my nightgown with my hands clamped around my head, I started crying as I tried to explain to my husband what had happened. I was in so much pain I could hardly talk coherently. After trying to make sense of my scattered explanation between sobs, he said, "Honey, we're getting you dressed and taking you straight to the hospital. Something is definitely not right."

I felt pretty helpless. I couldn't turn my head, couldn't bend over, couldn't raise my arms, or else the pain would shoot up my neck and into my scalp. So I had to surrender and let my husband dress me, all the way down to putting on my socks and shoes. Somehow my husband was able to get himself, our two girls, *and* me dressed in record time and into the car. He even had to buckle me into the car seat because I couldn't reach around to do it for myself.

As we drove to the hospital emergency room, again I thought to myself, *I don't get it. This is crazy. Why is my neck trippin' out like this?* After arriving at the emergency room and waiting for about twenty minutes, I was examined by a doctor. I was diagnosed with a severe neck spasm, probably from a pinched nerve, the doctor said. They gave me a neck brace, prescriptions for two different types of muscle relaxant pills, and an estimated four to five days' recovery time.

We stopped at the pharmacy to fill my prescription and then headed home. By the time we arrived home, I had decided not to pop any pills. Instead I wanted to explore this neck spasm's mental and emotional causes. What could it possibly be? I definitely needed to do some deep soul-searching and contemplation.

The first place I turned to was the back of Louise Hay's book to read up on the mental and emotional causes of neck-related physical dis-ease. There was a common theme to the neck-related issues: a refusal or resistance to turning to see or turning to face something. That evening, with these probable causes in mind, I managed to situate myself in front of my altar to seek clarity on what I was refusing to turn and face. I lit three candles, turned off the lights, and took three deep cleansing breaths in preparation for my meditation. I started my meditation by asking the Creator that the root causes of my neck spasm be revealed to me. I sat there quietly, breathing slowly and deeply, clearing my mind to make space for the answers to come. Gently and slowly an answer started to emerge, like a thick fog parting to reveal the image of a looming mountain that had been concealed.

As I sat there breathing slowly and relaxing deeper into my meditation, the answers continued to come. The message I received went something like this: *The neck spasm's first purpose was to get your attention.* I thought to myself, *Wow, God, you really know how to get my attention.* Next the message said, *You haven't turned to fully face the reality that you are going to land a* national *book contract. Your vision of having your book on bookshelves around the nation is going to become a* reality. *It is really going to happen.* There was a final piece in the message. The soft words whispering from my soul said, *Expect your book to be a success. But know that with success will also come tremendous responsibility. You must use the next six months to do the spiritual work on the areas of your character that still need further refining.*

This message resonated in my soul. I needed to realize that the series of miraculous events and coincidences that culminated in bringing my agent, my publisher, and me together were not accidental or circumstantial. They were part of divine order. Then I recalled how I had made comments several times over the months such as, "I can't believe this is really happening." I didn't realize how I was negating my blessings with these words of disbelief. I needed to realize that I was getting what I had been asking for since I was a little girl. I had been holding the seed of this vision for years, and now I was reaping the fruit. It was time for me to believe it, embrace it, and accept it, as well as recognize the *responsibility* of the blessing.

I knew that the message that came forth in my meditation was right on. As confirmation, the pain in my neck started to subside that same evening. By the afternoon of the next day my neck had regained 80 percent of its flexibility. I was able to dress myself, turn my head to the left and right, and even drive. With no pills or muscle relaxants, just doing the spiritual work. By the next morning there was only a slight twinge of pain in my neck. By the evening of the third day my neck had fully recovered, sooner than the doctor had predicted. In addition to healing myself of this neck spasm rapidly, I've also rapidly healed myself of sore throats, a bladder infection, and bronchial swelling using this same type of process.

The urgent times we're in call for us to start activating the inner healer, the inner physician that dwells within each of us. To help you become more familiar with the mental and emotional root causes of other dis-eases, I've listed a few areas of dis-ease that tend to be more common among Black women. I've also provided companion questions to help steer you in the direction of identifying possible underlying causes:

Back Problems

◦ where *don't* you feel "backed" or supported?

◦ Who or what do you need to "get off your back"?

◦ Are you holding "back" your love

Headaches

◦ Where are you being overly critical of yourself?

◦ Are you resisting the flow of life?

◦ Do you have some sexual fears?

Shoulder Problems

◦ Are you "shouldering" too much?

◦ Where do you feel overburdened?

◦ Are you delegating effectively or trying to do it all yourself?

Female Problems

◦ What men from your past are you still harboring resentment toward?

◦ Where are you suppressing or denying full expression of your femininity?

◦ Are you nurturing yourself?

◦ Where have you suffered a blow to your feminine self?

Weight Problems

◦ Are you regularly pampering and nurturing yourself?

◦ Where are you being denied love?

◦ Who has denied you love in the past?

◦ Are you still angry at one or both of your parents?

◦ What are you "weighting" for?

Eyesight or Vision Problems (for those who wear glasses or contacts or have cataracts)

◦ What aren't you willing to see?

◦ What don't you want to see?

◦ What are you afraid of looking at in your past, the present, or your future?

Stomach Problems

◦ What are you dreading or fearing?

◦ Where are you resisting something new?

◦ What aren't you able to "stomach" or digest in your life?

Feet Problems (the feet represent under-standing and grounding)

◦ Are you having trouble understanding yourself, a situation, or others?

◦ Where are you feeling off balance or misunderstood?

◦ Is there an area in your life where you feel you've lost your "footing"?

Skin Problems

◦ Where do you feel like you need to "break out"?

◦ Where do you feel anxious, worried, or threatened?

Conventional medicine's remedies for dis-ease and pain tend to be for temporary relief or to invade and remove whatever is *having* the pain, which isn't necessarily what is *causing* the pain and dis-ease. Conventional methods, however, often don't address the *source* of the pain and dis-ease or its underlying mental and emotional *causes*. They deal with the symptoms. Understanding that we have the ability to facilitate our body's self-healing process is empowering. This realization allows us to take back the power that we've given away to doctors. Reframing the role doctors play, from one of being an authority over our bodies to being facilitators of our healing, gives us the power to restore *ourselves* to a state of health. This is not to dismiss conventional medical methods, however. There are "life or death" situations where a dis-ease is so far advanced that a holistic healing method alone is no longer sufficient. Dis-ease can be healed, but you must be willing to change how and what you believe, act, and think.

Movement

A big factor that contributes to physical dis-ease is an insufficient amount of movement (new language, instead of *exercise*) in our daily lives. If we look at our day-to-day activities, we tend to move *only* enough to get us through each day. Our bodies are way too sedentary.

For the most part our daily movement consists of moving around our homes in the morning to get ourselves and others ready for the day. Moving to the car, into our place of work, and around the workplace. Then moving back to the car for the drive home. We may stop to do a few errands on the way home, but then we park as close to the entrance as possible so that we don't have to walk so far. Then we move around the house preparing dinner, doing housework, or tending to our families. We move back to bed! And then the cycle starts all over again the next day.

This may *seem* like a lot of bodily movement, but it's not. You'll notice that much of our daily movement is inside our homes, inside buildings, or inside stores or malls. If we were to strap a mileage odometer to our hips on an average day to track the amount of distance that we cover, we'd find ourselves averaging less than a half a mile a day. And to make matters worse, it's *inconsistent* start-and-stop movement. This is *not* enough movement to support our bodies in being and remaining healthy. We need to incorporate more movement into our lifestyle. And we need to incorporate movement activity that is *above and beyond* the movement required to carry out our daily activities and responsibilities.

Moving more in my life has certainly been an area of challenge for me. So I've started with baby steps. I started by incorporating more movement into my current daily activities. For example in the morning, first thing after getting out of bed, I do a minute of stretches. While I'm brushing my teeth, I do lunges and leg lifts. At night, before getting into bed, I do sit-ups. And instead of parking my car at the closest available parking space when I go to the store, I park farther away so that I can walk the extra distance. Here are a few suggestions for increasing the amount of movement in your life:

- Take a walk during your lunch hour.
- Walk a message to coworkers in your office instead of voice-mailing or E-mailing them.
- Take the stairs instead of the escalator at the mall or airport.
- Each morning take sixty seconds to stretch. Rotate your neck. Gently stretch up to the ceiling, down to the floor, and to each side.

◦ Walk to your mailbox to get the mail instead of picking it up when you drive by the mailbox.

◦ Power-walk up and down your hallway at home ten times every evening to get your heart rate up.

My ultimate goal is to build up to doing yoga or African dance at least twice a week, and walking at least once a week. I'm not there yet, but I'm working toward it. In the meantime I keep looking for ways to incorporate more movement into my daily activities. A body that doesn't move enough becomes filled with stagnant energy. Stagnant energy contributes to dis-ease. So the moral of this part of the story is to find ways to *move more* in your life!

SACRED PAMPERING PRINCIPLE FOR THE BODY #7— LAYING ON OF HANDS: THE POWER OF TOUCH

I remember how my mama's touch could calm my upset stomach or help my banged-up knee feel better. It seemed like Mama's hands had magical healing powers in them. She could lay a hand on my upset stomach, and a warm glow seemed to seep out of her hand into my stomach, dissolving the pain. This was amazing to me as a child, because at the time I didn't realize that Mama really was healing me with her hands.

Our hands are ideal vehicles for facilitating healing because they are movable, flexible, and portable. Their design and structure allow them to be excellent means for directing and redirecting the flow of energy through our bodies and the bodies of others. As mentioned earlier, our bodies have seven major energy centers, or chakras. Each chakra is like a radiating wheel of fine, subtle energy that permeates and extends out from our bodies.

If any of these energy centers become blocked or disharmonized, we become unbalanced, causing symptoms and malfunctions. A simplified definition of *healing* is "restoring balance, the uninterrupted flow of the body's vital energy so that a person is returned to a state of wholeness and well-being."

The New Testament is filled with stories of Jesus healing dis-eased people with a laying on of hands. Matthew 14:35–36 speaks of Jesus coming into the land of Gennesaret after feeding the five thousand with two fishes and five loaves of bread. And people from all over the land with dis-eases were brought to him. They only had to touch the hem of his garment and "as many as touched it were made perfectly whole." Matthew 15:30 says, "And great multitudes came unto him having with them those that were lame, blind, dumb, maimed . . . and cast them down at Jesus' feet, and he healed them."

In *Vibrational Medicine*, Richard Gerber, M.D., discusses a study that was conducted by Dr. Bernard Grad at the University of Montreal in the 1960s on the healing effects of the laying on of hands. Dr. Grad was interested in finding out if psychic healers had a real energetic impact on patients, above and beyond what might be due to belief and "charisma." He wanted to ascertain the true physiologic effects of emotion on living things.

As his subjects he chose plants instead of human patients in order to eliminate the known effects of belief (the so-called placebo effect). Grad first soaked barley seeds in salt water, which is a growth retardant, to create a "sick plant patient." Grad then had a healer do a laying-on-of-hands treatment on a sealed container with an equivalent mixture of salt water. Then he soaked a set of barley seeds in the "healer treated" salt water. The two sets of seeds, those soaked in the healer-treated water and those soaked in the untreated water, were then placed in an incubator and studied for signs of germination and growth.

Grad found that the seeds exposed to healer-treated water

sprouted more often than those from the untreated salt water. Even after potting the seeds and exposing them to equivalent conditions of growth, Grad discovered that the plants watered with healer-treated water grew taller and had a higher chlorophyll content.

Interestingly enough, in a similar experiment water energized by severely *depressed* patients had the reverse effect of healer-treated water in that *it suppressed the growth rate of the barley seeds*! After doing a chemical analysis of the healer-treated water Grad concluded that the healer was able to actually affect the electromagnetic charge of the water and thus the very water molecules themselves!

This same type of phenomenon is at work in our physical bodies. Our thoughts and emotions and their "charges" have a definite impact upon the electromagnetic field(s) of our bodies. These fields in turn foster health or dis-ease, depending on the kind of "thought diet" we feed our bodies.

Try this: Rub the palms of your hands together vigorously for a full ten seconds, then pull your hands apart slightly so that there is less than a half inch between them. Slowly move them slightly apart and then back together four times. Do you feel tingling or a sensation like a gentle force field? This is your body's energy field.

Massage

The laying on of hands is a practice that most of us are familiar with in the form of the basic massage. The word *massage* has its roots in the Greek word *massein,* which means "to knead." Massage therapy involves kneading a person's muscles and other soft tissue with the intent of improving his or her well-being or health. Massage is a practice that deserves deeper exploration. Its value goes beyond relaxation purposes to that of a therapeutic treatment. A therapeutic treatment is "one designed to treat disease or illness."

The back is the part of the body that tends to receive the most attention, but reframing massage as a therapeutic treatment requires that we look at other parts of the body as candidates for massage therapy. The extremities, the hands and feet, deserve more attention, especially the feet because they have a very high concentration of reflexology and acupressure points, with over one hundred nerve endings that correspond to specific body organs. Here is a brief listing of some general reflexology points of the feet, and the parts of the body to which they correspond:

Area of Foot	*Area of Body to Which It Corresponds*
Fleshy padded underside of each toe	Sinuses
Inner arch of right foot	Leg, knee, hip, lower back
Padded ball area of both feet	Lungs, chest, breast
Middle join of each toe	Hair
Inside contour of the feet between the big toe along arch to heel	Spine

A foot massage can revitalize your entire body because each foot has approximately fifty-five major reflexology points. A pedicure with a foot massage makes a wonderful combination.

Ancient and modern hands-on healing methods are making a comeback as people search for noninvasive therapies. These therapies, collectively known as bodywork and massage therapies, work with the body's vital energy system. Entire genres of massage therapies and bodywork healing modalities have reemerged. These hands-on healing therapies deal with unblocking stuck or stagnant body energy. These areas of congested energy show up in the form of bodily dis-ease, such as muscle tension, and stress-related conditions such as asthma, migraines, insomnia, and high blood pressure. To familiarize you with a few of the major bodywork therapies, I've included a few basic definitions.

Bodywork Modality	Description
Reiki	An ancient Tibetan healing system that uses light hand placements to channel healing energies to the recipient.
Acupressure	An ancient Chinese technique that involves the use of finger pressure (rather than needles) on specific points (meridians) along the body to treat ailments such as tension, stress, aches, pains, menstrual cramps, and arthritis.
Reflexology	With fingers and thumbs, practitioners apply pressure to specific points on the feet and hands that correspond to organs and tissues throughout the body.
Rolfing	Developed by biochemist Ida P. Rolf, this technique uses deep manipulation of connective tissue to restore the body's natural alignment, which may have become rigid through emotional trauma or injury.

Time and again scientific studies have shown that being touched increases our health and vitality. "Preemies," premature babies, who tend to have a low birth weight, are now receiving infant massage in many hospital nurseries. The preemies receiving regular massages show more rapid weight gain and responsiveness than those who didn't. Touching in the form of massage has not only general benefits but specific mental, emotional, and physiological ones as well. Below are some general benefits of therapeutic massage:

- Muscles gain elasticity and lose tenseness.
- Red blood cells increase, as well as the amount of hemoglobin in the bloodstream.
- Blood circulation is increased by the dilation of capillaries.
- Lymph flow is increased. Lymph, which is a key player in the body's immune system, is the bodily fluid that transports white blood cells.
- Massage raises skin temperature between four and five degrees, and even higher among women. The expansion of capillaries increases the nourishment of the glands and superficial tissues, producing a visible improvement in the appearance, complexion, and texture of the skin.
- Peripheral nerves are soothed by gentle stroking. Nerve endings actually tingle.
- The relaxing, sedative effect of general massage is the result of reflex responses of the central nervous system and may even produce sleep.
- The toxic by-products of muscular exertion, which cause fatigue, are eliminated more quickly following massage.
- Urine excretion is increased by general abdominal massage. The

percentage of nitrogen and sodium chloride (salt) excreted is greater after massage.

Doesn't it feel good when someone cups your face between their hands, strokes your arm, or gives you a warm bear hug? The reason these gestures of touch feel so good is that positive energy is being exchanged. We need to touch our men more, our children more, ourselves more! Especially since our society is moving more and more toward automation and high technology.

Touch is powerful and it can't be substituted. The warmth of the hand, the energy exchange, the sensation of the contact, the stroking and kneading do so much for our overall health, vitality, and aliveness. I'd recommend a professional body massage once a month if possible. If a professional massage is outside your means, then ask a lover, friend, or your husband to give you one.

SACRED PAMPERING PRINCIPLE FOR THE BODY #8— PAMPERING YOURSELF WHILE AT WORK

Those of us who are on a daily nine-to-five work schedule can also learn to incorporate pampering into our workday. Working a solid eight-hour day with only a break for lunch is a disservice to the mind, body, and spirit. Taking frequent breathers actually contributes to our productivity and effectiveness rather than detracts from it, as we might be led to believe.

If we wait until we get home to pamper ourselves, we're going too long without renewal breaks. So it is necessary to integrate ways to renew yourself into your workday.

Workday Pampering Tips

• Take your shoes off when you're at your desk and rub the soles of your feet together. Rotate your ankles. Wiggle your toes.

• Escape to the solitude of an empty meeting room in your building for lunch. Take a sack lunch and a good magazine or book with you to read.

• Keep a blanket or large beach towel in the trunk of your car. When the weather is nice, take your lunch break at a nearby park and stretch out on your blanket or towel.

• When you go to the park, take along a good book and a battery-operated cassette or CD player so that you can listen to a soothing tape while you relax on your blanket.

• Stand up occasionally at your desk when you are talking on the phone. Get a twenty-five-foot curly handset cord for your phone if necessary. Studies have shown that standing up while we are on the phone stimulates creativity and assertiveness, and also gets the blood flowing properly to your calves and feet.

• Keep a set of walking shoes or flats under your desk or in your desk drawer so that you can take a walk during one of your breaks for a change of pace.

• Get a manicure over your lunch hour.

• Go to lunch by yourself.

• Get a foot massage, face massage, or pedicure over your lunch break.

• Go to one of the full-service bookstores and find a quiet nook to read or relax. One of my favorite bookstores for this is Barnes & Noble. They have easy chairs and comfy couches in various locations around the store for your relaxing and reading pleasure.

- Keep affirmations in your desk drawer, on top of your desk, or on a wall at eye level so that your subconscious mind can absorb these positive messages throughout the day.
- If you have an office door, close it once a day for a five-minute "chill out" break. Do nothing. Don't take any calls. Put an IN A MEETING sign on your door if you have to so that you won't be interrupted.
- Bring a foot roller to work and keep it under your desk. Take your shoes off and roll the soles of your feet back and forth across it. (I got my foot roller from the Body Shop.)
- Make room for a small cassette or CD player on your desk or nearby on the floor. Play some "high-toned" soft jazz or nurturing music softly throughout the day. Keep the volume low so as not to disturb others or interfere with your phone calls.
- Keep a personal supply of refreshing herbal teas at your desk such as lemon orange or pepperiment. When you take your break, have a cup of herbal tea instead of coffee or a carbonated beverage.
- Treat yourself to a body massage over your lunch hour.

You probably have some other ideas that are now coming to mind—add your own to this list.

Rejuvenating Foot Soak

My final workday pampering tip is actually done at the *end* of your workday, once you've returned home. Once I get home after a particularly crazy day, I give myself a Rejuvenating Foot Soak.

To give yourself a Rejuvenating Foot Soak, run about two inches of warm water in your bathtub or in a plastic basin, just enough to cover the tops of your feet. Add a couple of drops of an energizing essential oil, such as orange, tangerine, or grapefruit, and ½ teaspoon of Epsom salts, if you have some on hand. (You can usually find Epsom salts at large grocery stores in their medicine or drug section.) If you're going to do your foot soak in your bathtub, fold up a towel and sit on it on the edge of the bathtub as padding for your bottom. Put your feet in the water and take three deep cleansing breaths. When you inhale, slowly say the word *peace* to yourself, and as you exhale, say the word *relax.* Wiggle your toes. Rotate your ankles. Rub the soles of your feet together. Rub the sole of one foot across the top of the other and then alternate. Soak your feet for a full five minutes. Cup your foot in your hand, turn up its underside, and press the pads of your thumbs into and around your arch area. When you are finished, dry your feet briskly with a towel. If you have some lotion or body oil, take two more minutes to rub some into each toe individually, rubbing the middle joint and squeezing the soft pad between your fingers as you do so. Mmm. It feels sooo good. Your entire body can feel rejuvenated after a foot soak because each foot is the site of over fifty-five major reflexology points.

SACRED PAMPERING PRINCIPLE FOR THE BODY #9— PAMPERING TOOLS AND SUPPLIES FOR YOUR JOURNEY

As you begin your journey to a self-caring lifestyle, you will want to be equipped with certain tools and supplies to support you. Some of the *basics* I suggest are candles, incense, an incense burner, scented bubble bath, and Epsom salts. My personal array of tools and supplies may include:

Supplies:

Fruit-scented bubble bath
Sea salt, which draws out the toxins and impurities from the skin (authentic Dead Sea salt is the best)
Scented Epsom salts and bath crystals, which soften the skin
Jasmine and lavender/tangerine essential oils
Scented body lotion
Honey almond soap
Scented body powder
Papaya body scrub and exfoliant
African musk soap
Incense (Somali Rose, African Love, Strawberry, Jasmine, Lavender, or Frankincense are my pampering bath favorites)
Perfume oils

Tools:

Body loofah
Back towel
Clay heel buffer
Natural body sponge
Body puff
Incense holder
Candles
Candleholders
Cassette/CD player (use one with "continuous play" so that you don't have to keep flipping over the tape)

If you enjoy listening to music during your pampering time, I suggest you choose music that is 60 beats per minute, to match your heart rate at rest. Some of the tapes I have in my collection are: *Sentimental Sax,* published by Northword Press, part of the "Nature Quest" series; *Iridescence I,* by Joel Andrews, produced by Search for Serenity; *From Heart to Crown* and *Miracles,* by Rob Whiteside-Woo; *Prelude to Lazarus,* by Synergy; *Fragrances of a Dream,* by Daniel Kobialka; *Forest Rain,* by Dean Everson, published by Soundings of the Planet; and music from Seattle-area musicians Susan Evans, Darren Motamedy, and Donald Johnson. I'm expanding my pampering music collection to world music and African healing drums.

Incense is important because every scent has its own particular vibration. This is why different scents can have different effects on you—the vibration differs from scent to scent. Smell is such a powerful sense because it registers directly and immediately in the brain. Smell is also a powerful memory trigger. Candlelight, too, has a gentle effect on the senses.

I suggest keeping an array of different-colored candles on hand because different colors also have different vibrations. This is why colors can have various affects and symbolic meanings. Here's a simple introduction to the properties of different colors and their impact upon our psyches:

Color	Property or Symbolic Meaning
Red	Sex, passion, love, energizing, warming, revitalizing
Pink	Romance, tenderness, new love, softening
Green	Appreciating of the body, realizing, harmonizing
Orange	Creativity and joy

Color	Property or Symbolic Meaning
Yellow	Cheering, uplifting, clarifying, dispels confusion
Blue	Peaceful, relaxing, cooling, balancing, calms emotions

It is helpful to know the properties and symbolic meaning of colors so that you can make use of this knowledge in your life, especially when it comes to your pampering and relaxation time. For example you may be challenged with a communication-related issue. Maybe you're upset with someone in your life and have something on your mind that's really bothering you but can't quite bring yourself to tell that person. During your meditation time it would be useful to burn a blue candle, which represents communication and self-expression. Or say you have an important decision to make and you feel like you're in a dilemma: During your meditation time it would be useful to burn a yellow candle, which represents clarity and dispels confusion.

Each of our body's chakras or energy centers is also associated with a different color. The following summary discusses the general qualities and characteristics of each chakra. Notice the colors of the seven chakras and how the qualities and functions of the chakras correspond to the properties of specific colors:

Chakra Color	Chakra Name	Qualities/Functions
Red	Root/Base	Earth, vitality, grounding
Orange	Sacral	Sexuality, sensuality, pleasure, procreation, desire, creativity, relationships

Chakra Color	Chakra Name	Qualities/Functions
Yellow	Solar Plexus	Will, vitality, personal power, identity, action, clarity
Green	Heart	Compassion, harmony, forgiveness, divine love, selflessness, healing
Blue	Throat	Communication, balance, self-expression, integrity, independence, wisdom
Indigo	Third Eye/Brow	Extrasensory perception, intuition, insight, clairvoyance
Violet/Purple	Crown	Bliss, integration, unity, enlightenment, purpose

You may want other tools such as an inflatable bath pillow, a journal with a cover that reflects your personality or the journal's purpose, a special writing pen, a special pillow or floor mat for sitting on during your meditation or altar time, and essential oils. Essential oils, like colors, bring about different effects. Essential oils are extracted from plants and flowers that have healing, medicinal, and therapeutic properties. Use a few drops of a particular essential oil in your pampering bath. Some of my favorites are:

Essential Oil	Characteristics
Citrus essential oils (orange, tangerine, grapefruit, lemon)	Stimulating and uplifting
Eucalyptus	Balancing and equalizing
Jasmine	Emotionally uplifting, cheering, promotes self-confidence and happiness, opens a "hardened" heart to the softness of love
Lavender	Appeasing and calming, an antidepressant
Neroli	Alleviates anxiety and nervous depression, a natural tranquilizer, calms and slows down the mind, purifies the blood
Ylang-ylang	An aphrodisiac (use very sparingly)

Other Calming Oils: Marjoram, chamomile, geranium.
Other Energizing and Stimulating Oils: Lemon, peppermint, clary sage (especially good for premenstral syndrome), pine, bergamot.

You also might try *perfume* oils. Perfume oil is more concentrated than over-the-counter perfume, which is mixed with large quantities of alcohol. The scent of perfume oils lasts longer on people of color due to the chemical composition of our melanin, the color-causing pigment in our skin. Three drops of perfume oil on key pulse points can last an entire day. If you don't have access to perfume oils, there are some available for order in the back of the book.

You can even use your perfume oil to make your own massage oil. Marcel Lavabre in the *Aromatherapy Workbook* offers a simple recipe. For every 12 ounces oil he suggests no more than ¼ ounce of essential oil or perfume oil. Oils that work well are sweet almond, canola, olive, peanut, corn, sesame, and sunflower. Be sure to store your massage oil in a bottle with an airtight lid to prevent degradation.

Getting your pampering tools and supplies together before your pampering bath may seem like preparation for a major production. Well, it is. And guess who's the special guest? *You!* You are worthy of this kind of preparation. I keep all of my pampering bath tools and supplies together in one place, in a big basket on the shelf in my bathroom closet, so that everything is easily accessible. If you were going to have guests over for dinner, there's a certain amount of preparation you'd put into it—grocery shopping for the food, cooking the meal, setting the table. So, shouldn't we be willing to put out the extra effort on *ourselves* when we are the special guest? If you want to take your pampering bath a step farther, ask your husband or partner to do your pampering bath prep for you, as an act of loving service to you.

Again, depending on my mood, I may also bring in one of my journals, a book, or a magazine to enjoy as I relax in the bathtub. Here's a little tip for scenting your water that you might want to use. Next time you go shopping at the mall or a department store, gladly accept the vials of perfume samples that are offered as giveaways. These samples can be collected and then poured into your bathwater to nicely scent it.

SACRED PAMPERING PRINCIPLE FOR THE BODY #10— SENSUAL LAYERING: WAYS TO ENHANCE YOUR PAMPERING EXPERIENCES

Sensuality is distinct from sexuality. The word *sensual* means "gratifying or appealing to the senses of sight, sound, smell, taste, and touch." *Sensual layering* or *sensual enhancing* are terms I use to describe taking a pampering experience and giving it greater depth and dimension by enhancing its sensual appeal. The objective is to maximize your pampering experiences so that they become multidimensional and sensually rich.

Let's take my weekly pampering reading as an example. I'll contrast the experience *before* sensual layering with *after*. *Before* sensual layering I might choose to retreat to my bedroom and recline comfortably on my bed to do some reading. To sensually enhance this pampering experience, I could prop myself up comfortably on the bed using my backrest; turn off my bright overhead ceiling light and turn on my bedside lamp for a softer effect; put high-toned, nurturing music on my cassette/CD player; burn lavender or rose incense; warm up my Cozy Comfy, my flexible, flannel-covered grain-filled wrap, and drape it around my neck and shoulders to relieve tension (you can get a similar version of a Cozy Comfy at Target stores in their body-care section); and prepare a cup of soothing herbal tea in my special jumbo teacup to sip while I read. With these simple enhancements a pampering activity can be transformed into a richer pampering experience by involving more of my senses. Another example of turning reading into a full pampering treatment is when I curl up on my living room couch with a certain blanket that has special appeal because of its warm, soothing autumn colors and its soft, fuzzy texture. And I pour a few drops of either vanilla, rose, apple, and lavender potpourri oil into the living room lamp's lightbulb ring and enjoy the relaxing, calming scent as the oil heats and evaporates into the air.

There are other simple, inexpensive ways to sensually upgrade your pampering activities. After taking a pampering bath put on a pair of pajamas or a nightgown that feels great against your skin. Switch from standard percale sheets to soft flannel ones. Smooth your body with a luscious fruit-scented lotion before climbing into bed. Instead of writing in your journal with a regular blue- or black-ink pen, use a beautifully colored designer writing pen or one that has an exotic color of ink, perhaps fuchsia, purple, or sky blue. Designer-look pens can be purchased for under ten dollars at most office supply and stationery stores. When you take your pampering bath, if you ordinarily have the bathroom light on, turn off the lights and bathe by candlelight instead. Use scented candles if you ordinarily use unscented. Try some exotic bubble-bath scents, such as papaya or mango, if you ordinarily use strawberry or peach.

Find ways to tickle your own fancy by sprinkling your life with little enhancements to nurture your spirit. Since writing is one of my joys, my pens and journals are part of my pampering treasures. I have a collection of special ceramic and designer writing pens for journaling or writing poetry. I also have five separate journals.

Look at your life to see where it can be touched up with gestures that add enrichment and pleasure. I keep one of my pampering-products baskets on the shelf in my bathroom closet and the other on my bedroom dresser. The basket on my dresser is filled with items such as scented body powder, scented body lotions and mousses, fruit-flavored (edible) massage balms, and exotic perfume-oil blends. The basket in my bathroom is filled with items such as sweet almond honey soap, scented stress-relieving bath crystals, mineral-bath packets, papaya bubble bath, coconut bubble bath, scented bath-oil beads, sea salt, Epsom salts, lavender and jasmine essential oils, a red clay buffing disk for my feet, and an assortment of manicure and pedicure supplies (see the back of the book for ordering information).

I have a little box I set aside especially for my collection of pampering music. I keep an assortment of beautiful stationery on hand for writing thank-you notes and letters to others and also an assortment of creative greeting cards for all occasions. Having greeting cards on hand allows me to send cards to friends and associates at the spur of the moment without having to make a trip to the store. I keep a felt-tipped calligraphy pen in my Wish Box so that I can write a name and address on an envelope in calligraphy instead of using my regular handwriting. Sometimes I'll slip an affirmation card or some tiny little foil hearts or stars into a thank-you card before I mail it.

I love fragrance, so I enjoy the soothing smell of potpourri oil as it warms in my light-bulb ring. Especially when guests are going to be coming over, I like them to be greeted at the door with delicious smells of either berry, apple, cinnamon, vanilla, or rose when they enter. It helps them feel at home immediately.

Five of my favorite places to browse and shop in Seattle for my pampering products are Basic Necessities, Soothing Sensations, Zanadia, Domaine, and The Soapbox. I especially like to take special trips to The Soapbox to buy extra-rich lotion to mix with their custom-blended perfume oils. I have a great time experimenting with the assortment of over forty different kinds of fruity, floral, woodsy, and exotic scents. I especially like to combine two oils together to create a unique "signature" scent. If you're not aware of a local pampering shop, try national and regional chains, such as The Body Shop, Garden Botanika, and even catalogs such as Avon and Jafra. Department stores likes JCPenney, Sears, Victoria's Secret, and Nordstrom now have sections devoted to pampering and body-care products. There are so many simple things in our daily lives that can become part of our personal pampering treasures. The important thing is to have fun with it and allow your full self to be expressed!

Our bodies are designed for sensual stimulation and they delight in experiences that appeal to multiple senses at once. Find simple ways to enhance your pampering experiences with layering. Ask yourself, *How can I upgrade this pampering experience to smell, taste, feel, look, or sound better?* Add fresh flowers at a meal. Play nurturing music while you bathe. Warm your massage oil before using it. Instead of just regular-style coffee mugs, I have jumbo-sized mugs in mustard yellow, white, and black especially for drinking my herbal tea when I'm pampering myself. I used to save my fancy crystal wineglasses for guests or holiday occasions. Now I use them for myself, for no particular reason except that I'm pampering myself. For example occasionally I'll decide to have a glass of sparkling cider, champagne, or fruit juice and drink it out of a fancy wineglass. Instead of celebrating a holiday I'm celebrating *me*. Our senses love stimulation and creativity, so experiment. Express yourself.

SACRED PAMPERING PRINCIPLE FOR THE BODY #11— PERSONAL PAMPERING: REFLECTIONS OF YOU

When, what, how, and where you choose to pamper yourself is as distinct and unique as you are. The pampering experiences you choose to indulge in should naturally reflect your personality, preferences, upbringing, childhood, family background, and likes and dislikes. This is why you want to allow yourself time to get in touch with your unique personal style. A closer examination of the *nature* of the experiences that bring you joy can give you valuable insights into yourself. You'll probably find that what you choose to do to pamper yourself is a deeper and fuller expression of who you really are and is also a reflection of your personal style.

As women our orientation is often toward accommodating and fulfilling others' needs to such a degree that we get out of touch with our own. So, discovering and exploring what brings you joy can be an exciting adventure into the deeper parts of yourself. Alexandra Stoddard in *Daring to Be Yourself* says, "True style is already within you and can be expressed. Find yourself by recognizing what gives *you* pleasure, what makes *you* feel good, what brings *you* delight."

Grant yourself permission to change your mind. Try new things. You may want to pamper yourself one way this month but switch to something else next month. Allow your pampering experiences to reflect your personal growth, mood, and current challenges at the time. Many of us are going through personal rites of passage and life transitions, and what we do to pamper ourselves can help facilitate our process. Sometimes you may want to indulge in quieter, calmer types of experiences, whereas at other times may want to do something wilder and more creative. Since pampering is a personal experience, you have the right to change, add, adjust, and delete items from your "What Brings Me Joy" list you created in Chapter 2 of this book.

In my Pampering seminars women have a chance to share their response to the question What brings you joy? Their responses are always delightfully diverse and varied because their responses are really holistic reflections of their individuality. Responses I've heard include writing thank-you letters; receiving sloppy kisses from my kids; watching the sun rise; writing a poem; having a good face-to-face conversation with my best girlfriend; staying in my pajamas all day; playing my piano; singing; sleeping in on the weekends; going to a concert; taking a relaxing, uninterrupted bath; getting a warm, bear hug; reading a good novel; having a slumber party; drinking a good cup of coffee; walking in the rain; and relaxing in front of a warm fire on a chilly evening.

Paying attention to the types of pampering activities and experiences you enjoy can reveal interesting aspects of your character and personality. What do these activities and experiences reveal about you? Do any of the following types of experiences apply to you?

Out-of-doors, back-to-nature experiences:
Hikes, nature walks, watching the sun rise or set, dangling your bare feet in a lake, bike riding.

Cozy, cuddly, stay-at-home experiences:
Snuggling on the couch or in your bed with a warm blanket and a good book. Enjoying a toasty fire and glass of champagne or a cup of tea. Staying in your pajamas all day.

Erotic, sensuous types of activities and experiences:
Oiling your body down and sleeping naked between the sheets. A body massage from a male masseur. Wearing silk or satin lingerie. Watching an erotic video in the privacy of your own home. Enjoying a hot tub or Jacuzzi.

Creative, artistic, inner-child experiences:
Fingerpainting. Coloring. Baking cookies. Building something with Legos. Making Play-Doh figures. Dancing around the house singing the *Sesame Street* or *Barney* theme song. Making a collage.

Carefree, self-expressed experiences:
Doing a "Chinese fire drill" at a stoplight. Rollerskating. A one A.M. breakfast date with your favorite girlfriends at a twenty-four-hour restaurant. Hosting a slumber party. Game night at your place with fun group games such as Pictionary, Scattergory, Charades, or Outburst.

The key is to add variety and continue expanding upon your pampering activities so that you don't get too complacent with the same types of activities and experiences. If you have a hard time branching out, make yourself a personal permission slip that says, "It's okay for me to try new things," and give it to yourself.

Through the process of allowing your pampering activities and experiences to change and expand as you change and expand, you'll stay in tune with your spiritual and emotional needs.

Much of what brings us joy has simply been "in remission" since our childhood. Pampering is also about getting in touch with activities and experiences from your childhood that brought you joy and pleasure. Here is a sampling of a few of the things from my childhood I've started doing again in the past several years:

• *Rollerskating*—I like the good old four-wheel-style rollerskates. Not those new in-line skates that are the current rage. I like to rent the speed skates when I go to the skating rink. They are sleeker and built closer to the ground. At the skating rink, when they make the call for the girls' fast skate, guess who jumps out there with the teenagers?

• *Making collages*—I like to keep issues of *Essence* and *Heart & Soul* magazines in a magazine basket next to my living room couch. Instead of just using them for future reference I now use them creatively to make personal collages. As a fun tool to assist me in feeding my mind a diet of powerful, healthy body images, I once decided to create a Body Temple collage. I cut out pictures of healthy, shapely, vibrant Black women and glued them onto a large piece of construction paper. Looking at these positive images of radiant, toned, voluptuous Black bodies helps to keep me on track and stay inspired. I keep my Body Temple collage on the bottom shelf of my altar.

• *Making greeting cards*—I keep large pieces of colored construction paper, plain white paper, colored markers, tape, glue, and artsy zigzag-edged scissors on hand in a special Art Box in my office. Instead of always purchasing my greeting and birthday cards at the store, I now hand-make some of them. I may cut out pictures of flowers, ethnic designs, or positive words and statements from magazines to glue on to my homemade cards. Sometimes I'll compose a poem especially for the individual receiving the card. My homemade cards have a more rustic look compared with the glossy store-bought versions, but the recipient always deeply appreciates them because he or she knows the card has been made with tender loving care.

• *Making gifts*—I decided to make a girlfriend's gift when she had her Divine Mate Empowerment Party. Instead of getting her a store-bought gift, I wanted to give her something special and unique. So I decided to make her a set of colorful five-by-seven-inch cards designed to help guide her on her journey to attracting her Divine Mate. Each card had a different theme, color, thought-provoking quote, and "self-work" assignment. For another girlfriend who had a Focus Empowerment Party, I bought a small decorated recipe box with a set of colored three-by-five-inch recipe cards. I cut out an assortment of powerful words and statements from magazines and glued them onto the cards along with a "recipe" on each one for achieving focus, maintaining clarity, and living *on purpose*. One day, months later when I was visiting her, I noticed she had posted one of her Focus Party "recipe" cards on her bathroom wall. This brought a big smile to my face and a warm feeling to my heart. I knew she was really putting the cards to good use.

SACRED PAMPERING PRINCIPLE FOR THE BODY #12—
THE MAGIC TOUCH: THE ART OF SELF-PLEASURING

If I asked you to stroke your cheek, touch your knee, stroke your thigh, or stroke your arm, you probably wouldn't hesitate. But if I asked you to stroke another part of your body—your clitoris— might you hesitate? Self-pleasuring has long been a silent taboo, especially for women, because it wasn't openly talked about when we were little girls or as we grew into young women. It was a hush-hush topic. But self-pleasuring can be a healthy and essential part of the pampering process.

I don't use the term *masturbate*. It sounds harsh and mechanical, so I choose to use the term *self-pleasuring*. Traditional religious doctrine has played a large part in casting a dark cloud over our passion and pleasure, especially self-pleasuring and self-stimulation.

The ability to have an orgasm is one of the Creator's most gracious gifts to us. Only a loving Creator would include a clitoris in the design of woman—the *only* organ in the human body devoted *entirely* to pleasure. How marvelous! Our vaginas are exquisite works of art. The clitoris is nestled at the top of your vulva, between the folds of the labia majora, the upper "lips" of your vagina, and is less than ¼ inch in size, but jam-packed with cosmic pleasure power. We must learn to appreciate the beauty and design of these marvelous organs.

Our genitals are a perfect combination of contrasting textures; they're self-lubricating, flexible, pliable, warm, moist, and compact. But we've received negative messages about touching and caressing ourselves over the years, which is one of the reasons we carry a lot of deeply buried shame and guilt about self-pleasuring. We must realize that every square inch of us is divine, including our genital organs. We have the authority to grant ourselves *full* permission to experience and enjoy sexual pleasure.

But many of us are not able to enjoy self-pleasuring fully because we are too preoccupied with self-criticism, being self-conscious, and are sexually shut down. Many factors block our ability to enjoy full sexual pleasure. Look at the programming we first received at home, at church, and from the media growing up. We need to recognize the many contradictions and negative messages that we absorbed around the issue of self-pleasuring.

Our parents wanted us to be "good girls." We were told to "keep our legs shut and our dress down." And "Do *not* get pregnant." In church we heard Bible passages interpreted to mean that it's sinful to be passionate and sexual. And that a sensuous woman is a sinful woman. In stark contrast to being a "good girl" was the other terrible possibility—that of being a "ho" or a "slut," the proverbial Jezebel. These inputs had the effect of wedging us between a rock and a hard place because we were presented with confusing contradictions. In between these two opposing images of the "good girl" on the one hand and the dangerous Jezebel on the other was a huge void. This void didn't seem to offer or explore any other options or choices. The power of these two opposing images was to create in us unconscious inner conflict.

In our minds the "ho" and "slut" represented the wild, openly passionate, expressive, uninhibited, orgasmic woman who didn't have a problem self-pleasuring. The "good girl" represented the "decent" Christian woman. But in our minds she also represented the boring, sexually inhibited, sometimes-orgasmic or orgasm-faking type of woman. So secretly we desired the *experience* of the Jezebel-type woman. We admired her freedom and daring. She wasn't afraid to have orgasms. And she wasn't afraid to try new positions or creative techniques. The "good girl," we silently concluded, *didn't have any fun.*

So we grew up in a state of *inner conflict.* Our *internal* desire was to be wild, sexy, orgasmic, and passionate. But our *external* conditioning told us that we had to be decent "good girls." With these limited options we didn't see how we could have it all—be "good girls" *and* be uninhibited, passionate, and orgasmic. This place of balance that lies between the two extremes hadn't been presented to us.

I think the reason that many "good girls" rebel, become loose, and go sexually out of control as they get older is because it is the only way they see to reconcile these two extremes and to experience the full sexual pleasure that they so much desire and appreciate. Because of the Jezebel image lingering in their subconscious mind, they believe they have to abandon the "good girl" image *altogether.*

Several important pieces were missing from the inputs we received about sex and self-pleasuring growing up. These missing pieces created an imbalance in our psyches that in turn affected our outlook and attitudes toward sex and self-pleasuring. These missing inputs include the following:

- The permission to be both a "good girl" and sexually expressed, passionate, uninhibited, and orgasmic
- An emphasis upon the balance that lies between the two extremes of "good girl" and "slut"

- Dialogue about our bodies as deserving of and designed to receive pleasure
- A view of sexual pleasure as positive, natural, and healthy; and self-pleasuring as positive, natural, and healthy; and that touching, exploring, and stroking your body, including your vagina, is okay
- Self-pleasuring as a path to awakening the sensuous woman within

Our education about sexuality was limited, for the most part, to a lesson in health class that covered the reproductive organs and sexually transmitted diseases. For many of us the extent of the conversations we had with our parents, our moms in particular, had to do with our beginning to menstruate. The part about our bodies being divine and sacred was missing. The conversation about it being okay to touch and explore our bodies, to find out what feels good to us, was missing.

This is why it is necessary for us to undo the negative programming we received as little girls and during our teenage years. The following exercises can help you get rid of some of the stigmas you may be carrying around about your sexuality:

• *Have a sensuality chat session*—talking about sexuality and eroticism within the safe environment of a sistercircle can help loosen up feelings of embarrassment, guilt, or shame you have around issues of sex. The more you discuss it openly, the freer you'll feel. Have an evening sistercircle session where the topic is sexuality and eroticism. Have everyone bring their own coffee cup and you provide the low-fat popcorn and the tea.

Also have each friend bring her favorite erotic stories; these may be excerpts out of *Erotique Noire,* a collection of erotica written by Black writers; *Herotica,* a collection of erotica written by women; a juicy love scene out of "Arabesque," the line of Black romance novels; *Pleasure,* by Lonnie Barbach, Ph.D., another collection of erotica written by women; *Delta of Venus,* erotic short stories by Anaïs Nin; or even Danielle Steel's *Princess Daisy.* That novel has a fireside love scene that I read ten years ago and still remember to this day. You can start the evening by having members of the circle read their favorite excerpt. Afterward you can talk about the excerpts or have a fun discussion around a question like "What do you think is the sexiest part of your body?" or "What is one of your sexual fantasies?" You can also try writing out questions in advance on small pieces of paper and putting them in a bag to be pulled. Everyone takes a turn at answering one of the questions.

• *Write an Erotic Story*—another way to loosen up the sexual stigmas is to write your own erotic story. Be detailed and expressive. Break it down. Describe it step by step. Avoid using general statements like "Then we made love." Instead try something like this: "His warm, moist mouth and probing tongue covered my nipple, and he licked and sucked it like a melting ice-cream cone. Then he . . ." Got the idea? The story can be for your eyes only, so write it with no holds barred. It can be either completely fictitious or based upon an actual experience—whatever works for you.

Discovering and delighting in your body is a rite of passage that enables you to more fully enjoy sexual pleasure with a partner. For women especially, shame-free self-pleasuring naturally opens the door to more fulfilling and gratifying sexual experiences with a partner. At the same time, self-pleasuring also helps you know the intimate terrain of your body better. Discovering your intimate terrain means exploring your distinct curves, the feel of your skin, the shape of your breasts, the curve of your butt, and all the rest of your body's textures and sensations.

Our bodies are almost always concealed by clothes, so we rarely get to enjoy our naked bodies in *full* view, besides catching a glimpse of ourselves in the mirror as we get in or out of the shower or bathtub. It can be rare for us to touch our bodies with our bare hands, since a washcloth or bath towel often prevents direct contact between our hands and our skin. Exploring your intimate terrain gives you healthier "body esteem."

Being able to pleasure yourself demonstrates a certain level of body acceptance and level of comfort with your sexuality. But releasing ourselves from the bondage of our past programming and conditioning and the images that we associate with touching ourselves "down there" may take some time. Be gentle and patient with yourself. Take a few minutes to make some notes about some of the inputs you received about self-pleasuring, then write a specific self-affirming statement for each to counter the negative programming.

Messages I Received About Self-Pleasuring	New Positive Imputs
1. *Example:* Only "hard up" women self-pleasure.	1. *Example:* Self-pleasuring is about self-discovery and sensuality.
2. _____	2. _____
3. _____	3. _____
4. _____	4. _____
5. _____	5. _____
6. _____	6. _____

Were the messages positive or negative? How have these messages affected your behaviors and attitudes around the issues of self-pleasuring? If you haven't tried self-pleasuring before, ultimately the most effective way to move beyond these disempowering beliefs and any shameful associations you may have is simply to do it.

Sometimes the most challenging aspect of self-pleasuring isn't the act itself, it's carving out times and places for yourself where you feel secure and safe from interruption. With so many demands on your time and energy, there may not be much time and space for privacy. A roommate, kids, or your husband can make it difficult to set up an uninterrupted opportunity for self-pleasuring. However, if you are *really* interested in exploring self-pleasuring for the first time, or in exploring it more fully, you'll find a way to make it happen. You may have to get a lock for your bedroom door. You may have to come home early from work or come home during your lunch hour. Do what you need to do to make it happen for yourself if this is something you sincerely want to explore.

Arrange your self-pleasuring setting as if you were planning a sensual evening with a lover. In this case *you* are the lover. Give yourself at least forty minutes for your self-pleasuring session. You don't want to be rushed. Some of the sensual enhancements you may want to have are candles and soft music. You'll also need some body oil. Avoid using lotion if possible, because oil provides a better feel and "glide." Next you'll need what I call an arousal enhancer—a feather, scarf, handkerchief, tie, or soft piece of fabric will do. The arousal enhancer is something you can hold in your hand to use as a tingling prelude to stimulating yourself with your hand. It heightens your sensitivity to touch. If you like, you may choose to use an aid, such as a vibrator—that's cool too. Whatever tickles your fancy, or better yet, whatever tickles your clitoris.

Choose the time and place, and set a sensual mood for yourself. Light some scented candles and African Love incense if you have some, and turn down the lights. You may first want to take a shower or bath with a sexually stimulating essential oil such as ylang-ylang. Take several nice slow, deep cleansing breaths to clean out stale air and help relax your body. Your place of choice for your self-pleasuring may be on your bed, a futon, a couch, or lying on a soft blanket on top of a carpeted floor. Slightly elevate your head with a pillow to ease pressure on your lower back. Be sure your oil and arousal enhancer are close at hand. If you are also going to enjoy music on a cassette/CD player, be sure it is in "continuous play" mode so that you don't have to stop and turn a tape over or change a compact disc.

Okay, so now you are ready to indulge. Lie back slowly with your legs parted. Adjust your body so that you are comfortable. To slow your breathing down and to relax further, take five deep, gentle breaths, inhaling and then exhaling in the full count of three. If your exhalation is "choppy" instead of smooth and flowing, take a couple more deep breaths—you need to relax more. Pour some of your body oil into the palm of your hand and rub your hands together briskly for a full ten seconds. Place your right hand over your heart—your fourth chakra—and your left hand over the area slightly below your navel—your second chakra.

Focus on the gentle rise and fall of your abdomen with each breath. Rub your hands together again briskly. Slowly run your fingertips up over your stomach; over your breastbone; up across your neck, cheeks, eyes, and forehead; and then all the way back down again. Run your full hand over the outside of your thighs, the inside of your thighs, up and down your arms, and then up over your breasts and back down. Do this three times. Each time go back to your relaxing breaths. You may notice that your breathing is quickening. So take two deep breaths to relax again. Now pick up your arousal enhancer. Starting on your right side, slowly sweep the arousal enhancer up your right thigh, across your stomach, over your right breast, across your face, across your forehead, and back down your left side, ending near your left thigh. Repeat this entire process, now going from left to right. Feel your nerve endings respond to the contact. Feel your body tingling as you lovingly and lightly sweep it. Do the body sweep a couple more times. Then put down the touch enhancer and take a couple more deep breaths.

Place the palm of your hand over your lower stomach area so that it rests 1 to 2 inches below your navel. Let your fingertips rest against the labia majora, the upper lips of your vulva area between which your clitoris is nestled. Place the other hand on your breast so that your fingers are resting on the nipple. Start gently and rhythmically to drum your fingertips against the lips of your vagina. Alternate between drumming, stroking, and gently making small circles around your clitoris and your vagina's lips as they start to moisten. Take a deep breath.

You may want to lick your fingertips and then brush them back and forth over nipples at the same time. Run your middle finger or both your middle and ring or index fingers around and around the inner rim of your vulva's lips and back and forth across your clitoris. If you start to get aroused too quickly, slow down your stroking, your drumming, and your breathing. This ebb-and-flow, crescendo-and-decrescendo pacing helps to build the ecstasy and prolong your pleasure. Try brushing your fingertips back and forth horizontally across your clitoris. Continue to alternate between this back-and-forth motion and a circular motion until you find the stimulation that feels best to you. Try slipping two fingers inside your vagina and experience its wetness and smooth texture.

Again, if your arousal starts to build, slow down the stimulation and take a couple of deep breaths. These breaths help to "pull" the pleasure up to the upper parts of your body. Then resume your stimulation. This time, just as you feel you're about to reach orgasm, suck in a slow, deep breath as your pleasure continues to build up. When you've reached the limit of your inhalation, begin to release the breath with as much sound as possible. Really sing out. The volume of your sound influences the depth of your orgasm. After you come to orgasm, take a couple of deep breaths to relax again. Whisper a simple affirmation to yourself: "Yessss."

To add to your self-pleasuring experiences, try new things. Start your self-pleasuring session by visualizing a fantasy in full color, sound, taste, smell, and touch. Act out your sexual fantasies inside the privacy of your mind. Maybe use an arousing video or read some tasteful erotica to set the mood. Give yourself permission to get creative.

In addition to providing pleasure, which is an end in itself, orgasms have emotional and physiological benefits as well, according to an article in the March 1996 issue of *Heart & Soul*. Endorphins (the body's tranquilizing chemicals secreted by the brain) also are released during an orgasm, which helps to strengthen your immune system. Orgasms can also help to ease tension headaches; they help pump up the endocrine system, which manufactures the body's hormones; and they can help you to be more spontaneous and less inhibited.

5

GUILT AND OTHER TRIPS

The self-work and inner work that go into pampering are only part of the adjustments that take place on the journey to a self-caring lifestyle. The other part of this shift involves *others* in your life. Be aware that feelings of guilt may creep in as you actively start shifting your lifestyle and priorities.

After behaving and acting a certain way for a long time, others become accustomed to your behavior. They learn how to relate and interact with you based on these familiarities. In fact they count on you to consistently present to them the Self they've come to know. Those who have become the most comfortable with the former you are those who stand to be the most accommodated by your "self-last" mentality. These are also the same ones who can be the most disturbed or upset by your new order of priorities. They are used to you directing your attention toward them, not toward yourself. Their comfort zones have been erected around the Self they've known you to be.

In *Sisters of the Yam: black women and self-recovery,* bell hooks shares the reaction her sister experienced from her family when self-care became a priority in her life:

> When one of my sisters, who has a husband and family, began to place "care of the self" on her agenda, her changes were greeted with familial rage and hostility. Considering that it was her practice to rush home from work and without even taking a moment's rest to begin meeting the demands of everyone, particularly fixing meals, it is not surprising that it was a shock to the family.

So it would do you good to prepare yourself *in advance* for possible "fallout" from loved ones and friends as they adjust to your new disposition and attitude.

Overcoming Guilt

Shifting to a self-caring lifestyle is about giving yourself permission to be free of your personal history, old programming, and old ways of thinking, acting, and *being*. In my Pampering seminars I continue to remind women of an old Chinese proverb: "State your position, and others will adjust accordingly." If you've been living your life from a Bottom-of-the-Priority-Pole, self-last mentality and you decide it's time you moved to a more empowering position, it's only natural that those who have always been above you on your Priority Pole will feel threatened and possibly offer some resistance. There may be some initial negative, unsupportive reactions from family and friends, so prepare yourself. Don't worry. They'll get over it. They don't yet realize that your self-care-first attitude benefits them too. Be patient and compassionate, but be firm.

To better understand the feelings of guilt you might experience during your transition, it would be useful to distinguish between what writer Cat Saunders describes as the "should guilt" versus the "good guilt" syndrome. She explains that "should guilt" typically arises when you break *someone else's* rules about how you "should" act. "Good guilt," however, is usually triggered when you break one of your *own* rules. Be aware that you may experience a lot of "should guilt" during your transition phase from your old lifestyle to one that is more balanced and integrated with pampering.

To offset the guilt you may be feeling, you may *subconsciously* try to sabotage your pampering efforts, or allow others to do so. *Don't go there.* When you are making a transition to a new way of thinking, behaving, acting, and being, your old beliefs and thoughts still have a grip on you. And they will probably resurface and try to catch you off guard by trying to trip you up with guilt.

PHASES OF THE TRANSITION

The Transition Phase is the stretch of this journey between how and where you *were* and the pampered and nurtured woman that you're *becoming*. The Transition Phase can be bumpy because how you've acted in the past is what others are familiar with and used to. Self-care is an ongoing process, and it is one that seems to go through several distinct stages. If I were to summarize the path to integrated self-care into a process, it would flow something like this:

Stage	*Characteristics and Indicators*
Experiencing the Void	You're tired of the daily grind. You discover there is not enough joy and pleasure in your life. You are not feeling fulfilled. You feel that there has got to be more to it than this. There's lots of activity and "doing" in your life. You may be feeling stuck or experiencing a temporary period of depression.
Self-reflection and Inner Stirrings	Restlessness. You don't know where to begin or how to get started, but you're clear that some things need to change or shift in your life. You start to think about what is and isn't working. You see the light, but may not quite know how to reach or connect with it.
Decisiveness and Inner Change.	You decide to do something about how you feel. You decide to be "at cause" instead of "at effect." You're getting clear on needed changes in attitude, priorities, behavior, and thinking. You are ready to start shifting. You've made a commitment to change.

Stage	Characteristics and Indicators
Early Action and Early Change	You're beginning to think differently. You're starting to embrace new perspectives on yourself and on pampering. In your mind you've begun to move yourself to a higher slot on your Priority Pole. You may be using affirmations, new language, visualization, and doing the spiritual work to heal yourself. You've successfully accomplished four or more planned pampering activities. Self-care is beginning to show up in your life.
Evidence and Outer Change	There is now a space between where you were and where you are going. This is perhaps the most challenging phase. You are on the grow. Others are taking notice of the changes you're beginning to make, and some may even comment. You may be experiencing resistance from others. You are sticking to your personal pampering schedule. You have a new attitude that is showing up in your actions, behavior, and decisions.

Stage	Characteristics and Indicators
Arrival	You have a new pace, new boundaries, a new outlook, and a new perception on pampering that is empowering. You're embracing new thoughts and beliefs about yourself and your body. You are consistently pampering yourself. You may look different. You are experiencing "fullfillment" of the void.
Integration	Self-care is a reality. Pampering is woven into the fabric of your life. You consider it necessary maintenance. You are experiencing real results. Your life is a reflection of self-care and more balance. You don't need the structure of a personal pampering plan anymore because now self-care is naturally built into your lifestyle. Your appearance has changed for the better.
Expansion and Evolution	Your influence on others is being felt in positive ways. Pampering with a partner may be in the transition or integration phase. Other areas of

Stage	Characteristics and Indicators
Expansion and Evolution *(continued)*	your life are transforming too. Your friends and spouse are being positively affected. You are continually moving to higher and deeper levels of wholeness, spiritual growth, and "in-joyment" in your life.

There are certain degrees of vulnerability you have in the Transition Phase, especially during the "Evidence and Outer Change" stage. Guilt is a by-product of the breakup of old limiting ideas, belief systems, and feelings of being obligated to compulsive over-nurturing and accommodation of others. This is why sabotage at this phase is highly likely—sabotage by others *and* self-sabotage. Heads up, because sabotage can sneak up on you.

For example, your little girl may *suddenly* "have to go pee" as soon as you shut the bathroom door and get comfortably settled into your pampering bath, even though you just asked her minutes earlier if she had to go and she assured you she didn't. Or, at the last minute, your husband remembers an all-important game on TV he just *has* to see the same night as your pampering time, even though you had cleared it with him days before and he had agreed to watch the kids.

Heads up for self-sabotage too. You may allow something or someone to infringe upon your previously planned pampering time. What appears to be an emergency may arise to "conveniently" interfere with your pampering plans or cause you to cancel them altogether. Be firm, because it's critical that you be very clear about pampering's importance in your life. You have to take a stand for your personal well-being.

If you are still uncertain and shaky about asserting this, others will be able to sense it and pick up on your uncertainty. And knowingly or unknowingly, they may exploit this soft spot. Be aware of comments such as, "Mama, you never used to . . . ," or "I don't like this new self-care thing you're into." Others are *much* more self-sufficient than we acknowledge or *allow* them to be. Remember, taking a firm stand for your own well-being is *not* self-centered. Being self-centered is a *self-only* attitude, while pampering is a *self-care-first* attitude. This is a major distinction. Healthy self-love requires that you first tend to your own needs so that you are at your best when tending to the needs of others.

During your Transition Phase also be aware that some of your old stuff may come up. Your "old stuff" consists of thoughts about pampering being selfish; allowing yourself to fall back into an overworked, overcommitted pattern again; having a hard time using the *N*-word (*no*), or allowing your boundaries to be violated. "Old stuff" is any negative, limiting thought that keeps us from pampering ourselves regularly. That's okay. It doesn't mean that you're reverting. Allow it to come up *and* let it pass on by. Recognize it for what it is, let it go, and *stay your course*. Stay clear. Stay focused. Return to your affirmations to help refortify yourself.

If pampering starts to feel like a chore or it becomes a little stressful trying to carve out sacred time, it's probably time to take a step back and reassess. This is a sign of pampering possibly slipping into the "another thing to do" category. This is a red flag.

Pampering shouldn't *take* your energy, it should *rebuild* and *renew* it. So if it starts being a pain to "work it in" or you keep missing your pampering dates with yourself, stop and take a step back. What are these dynamics the symptom of? Are Pampering Gremlins on the loose in your life? Do you have a major issue or decision that you are avoiding? Spend some time doing some soul-searching if any of these red flags are waving. To help you get back on track, choose a simple pampering activity that is easily doable and write it in your calendar. For example, "Wednesday night—ten minutes of relaxing reading before going to sleep." Keep rebuilding slowly, taking it a baby step at a time if you have to.

The following affirmations were specifically developed to help counter the deep-seated thoughts and beliefs that can resurface to sabotage your self-care efforts. Feel free to create your own affirmations. These should help you get started.

Challenge	*Affirmation/New Programming*
Self-sabotage	I am worthy of being pampered.
	Self-nurturing fortifies my mind, body, and spirit.
	I successfully complete my personal pampering plans.
	I manage my time and energy so that I am able to honor my self-care needs.
	My personal pampering time is a priority.
	I keep my word to myself.

Challenge	Affirmation/New Programming
Sabotage by others	Family and friends see my pampering as self-service that ultimately benefits them too.
	Family and friends support me in keeping my pampering commitments to myself.
	I am more attentive and responsive to the needs of others when my own needs are met first.
	I am a better (fill in the blank) (*mother, wife, writer, consultant, friend, employee, speaker*) when I nurture myself regularly.

"Retraining" Family and Friends

There are certain tools and aids you can use to assist loved ones in *their* evolution as you move through your process. And it isn't just those *inside* the home who can be affected by your "adjustments"; it can also be people *outside* your home who have grown accustomed to a certain you and may offer some resistance. This includes relatives, coworkers, neighbors, friends, church members, or a boss or supervisor.

If you have children of reading age, I suggest making a simple DO NOT DISTURB (DND) sign to hang on your doorknob. You can use your sign when you are relaxing, praying, meditating, bathing, reading, or having your Quiet Time. It serves as a signal to let them know that your personal pampering time is to be honored and respected. And in the meantime emergencies and crises will have to be put on hold or handled by someone else.

Your children will probably find this DND sign very intriguing. They may try to test you to see if you're really serious about not allowing interruptions. They may knock repeatedly on the door while calling out your name, or try to engage you in a conversation through the door. They may knock on the door saying, "Mama, what are you doing? Can I come in?" A good way to avoid these "innocent" attempts at interrupting you is to explain to them *in advance* that you are taking some pampering time. Let them know approximately how long you'll be *and* why your pampering time is important to you. Get them squared away *beforehand* so that all hell doesn't break loose as soon as you close your bedroom or bathroom door. If they can get you to allow an interruption the first few times you're in DND mode, they know they've got you. So you must stay firm.

Another tool for helping retrain family members is getting a magnetic calendar for the refrigerator so that all family members have a visual reminder of your pampering plans. In addition to scheduling other family activities, use the calendar to mark off the days you've reserved for your personal pampering. You can use a code such as P.P.T. (Personal Pampering Time), M.S.R. (Mom's Solitary Refinement), or simply put an X in the date box on the calendar. Be sure all family members are clear on the meaning of your calendar codes.

CREATING A SUPPORT SYSTEM

This third suggestion works especially well for those who are solo parenting. Set up a mutual exchange arrangement with another solo parent. Once or twice a month alternate watching each other's kids for two or three hours. This break gives you a chance to have regular monthly pampering time that you can count on. It is also useful to develop two or three baby-sitter relationships so that you have backups.

My husband and I have four different baby-sitters. They are part of our support system. When I was nearing the manuscript deadline for this book, I had a baby-sitter come to our home for the weekend to take care of Adera and Kiana while I worked in my office, since my husband also had to work at the same time. This allowed the girls to be here at home while I was in my office typing, and I didn't have to be concerned with packing them up and taking them to someone else's house for the weekend.

Or give yourself pampering time in the evening. Get the kids to bed an hour early so that you can have the rest of the evening to yourself. Get the support you need to stick to your plan. Maybe you need a reliable friend to call you at home thirty minutes before your pampering time begins to ensure that you follow through and stay on course. If you decide to do this, be sure the girlfriend you ask is demonstrating a commitment to self-care in her own life. Otherwise she may not fully understand the importance of her reliable support.

Sometimes it's not the kids who need the most retraining, it's our girlfriends. We have to let them know, too, that our pampering time is sacred. Often our friends expect us to always be accessible. They can be resistant when you become more protective of your time and energy.

Let's say you've set aside a particular Friday night for some personal pampering time. You inform your best girlfriend a couple of days earlier that this Friday night is going to be your pampering night and you won't be available to go out. Nonetheless she ignores this and tempts you with an invitation to go out on the town. Whether you stay your course or decide to take her up on the invitation will send a message to her about the *real* importance of your pampering time. It is very important that you keep your word to yourself. Your date with yourself is just as important. The "town" will still be there next weekend, but your peace of mind may not.

Family, friends, a coworker—they *all* have the ability to adjust. Your shift may seem to disrupt their lives *temporarily,* but they'll get over it. What you'll probably notice is that it's their *resistance* to your changes and transitions that are making it such a big deal for them, not your *actual* changes and transitions.

6

WHERE THE RUBBER MEETS THE ROAD

The most rewarding aspects of shifting to a self-caring lifestyle are the *real, visible* results. I continue to be amazed at how apparent it is when a woman *regularly* pampers and nurtures herself. I've seen women go through a literal metamorphosis—myself included—as a result of making this shift. One of the most obvious results is my successful and permanent release of almost forty-five pounds over the past five years. I attribute this directly to my shift in priorities, attitudes, thoughts, and beliefs about the value of self-care. The Debrena of today is very different from the Debrena of a few years ago.

CREATING A PERSONAL PAMPERING PLAN

In the early phases of transition to an integrated self-caring lifestyle, I've found that it's helpful to have more structure and conscious planning than you might ordinarily require. I suggest using your calendar, appointment book, or organizer for your pampering planning. One of the keys to achieving a truly self-caring lifestyle and seeing powerful results in your life is the ability to *incorporate* pampering into your daily and weekly life schedule. Pampering should be consciously integrated into your life, not squeezed in when you have spare time. Pampering is not intended to be a sporadic, fly-by-night undertaking—it should be a regular priority.

If you find yourself struggling to "make" time or "find" the time, consider changing your mind-set from a focus on *time* to a focus on better managing your *energy*. Take an honest look at how you are using your energy. What kinds of things and circumstances seem to come up or interfere with your pampering plans? A little extra structure in the form of a schedule can help you stay on course, especially if: (a) pampering is new to you; (b) you are a busy woman; (c) you are employed by someone else; (d) you are a procrastinator; or (e) you are prone to self-sabotage or sabotage by others.

The first step of structuring your pampering plan is to get out your personal calendar or organizer if you have one. Depending on your schedule, you may look one or two weeks ahead for planning purposes, whichever works best for you. Select one day of the week as your day for one full hour of pampering. Put an X in the box so that, at a glance, you can easily identify the day(s) you've set aside for your personal pampering. Also write in the actual time of the one-hour block that you want to set aside for your pampering (e.g., eight to nine P.M.), just as if it were a scheduled appointment. Which it is, an appointment with yourself!

I have a month-at-a-glance calendar. And at the beginning of each new month I mark off my days for pampering. I designate two evenings as my pampering bath nights, and two Fridays a month as my pampering days. Since I am self-employed, I am fortunate to have a high degree of control over my daily schedule. I work hard, so I feel that I deserve plenty of pampering. It keeps me balanced. I give a lot to my family, my community, my friends, my business, and my audiences when I speak, so I need plenty of pampering to renew myself. I'm working toward every Friday during the day being *totally* devoted to personal pampering and "play," but I'm not quite there yet. And Friday nights are designated as partner pampering times for me and my husband (more on partner pampering a little later).

Once you schedule your pampering time, stick to it. Keep your word to yourself. This is important, especially in the early phases of your transition so that you can establish a pattern of excellence and lock into a life tempo that naturally incorporates time for pampering. When you are planning your personal pampering time, turn back to the "What Brings Me Joy" list you created earlier, and incorporate these items into your pampering plan. Here are some other general ideas to stimulate your creative juices:

1. Write a love letter to yourself, and mail it back to yourself.
2. Paint your toenails if you usually don't.
3. If you do, try a new color.
4. Take a day trip by yourself.
5. Turn off the ringer on your telephone and let your answering machine field your phone calls for at least three hours.

6. Give yourself a pedicure.

7. Let a professional give you a pedicure if you usually do it yourself.

8. Make a "goals and dreams" collage using cutouts from magazines.

9. Have your significant other write you a love letter and read it to you.

10. Read a Black romance novel while enjoying a cup of herbal tea.

11. In the morning brush your teeth by candlelight.

12. Visit your favorite cosmetic counter at the department store and have the representative give you a free makeover.

13. Collect vials of perfume samples to pour into the water of your pampering baths.

14. Take a walk by yourself.

15. Sleep in.

16. Stay in your pajamas all day.

17. Go to a Saturday matinee movie by yourself.

18. Start a pampering piggy bank. Donate to it each week. At the end of the month treat yourself to a pampering experience.

19. Send a thank-you letter.

20. Eat a meal with your opposite hand (i.e., your left hand if you're right-handed) so that you slow down and savor each bite.

21. Try a new hairstyle.

22. Laugh, laugh, laugh!

23. Give out three full body hugs in one day.

24. Create a personal altar.

25. Make a homemade set of affirmation cards.

26. Sit still for twenty minutes, doing nothing.

27. Stretch out spread-eagle on your back, on your bed, with your head at the foot of the bed, for twenty uninterrupted minutes.

28. Host a sisterfriends slumber party.

29. Have a foot-massage party.

30. Have an Empowerment Party for yourself and ask a friend to hostess it.

31. Get into your pajamas as soon as you get home from work.

32. Have a family member or your spouse make you breakfast in bed.

33. Go on a solo nature hike.

34. Take a day off from work to pamper yourself. Instead of a sick day call it a renewal day.

35. Stay at home and relax for an entire weekend.

36. Have a friend over for some good conversation and sit on the floor for a nice change of pace instead of in chairs or on the couch.

37. Browse through a bookstore, and take your own sweet time.

38. Take a shopping trip for personal pampering tools and supplies.

39. Listen to a motivational tape while you drive to work.

40. Take a fun, onetime adult education course at a local community college or through an extension program.

41. Try out an alternative to a gym or health-club workout, such as yoga, t'ai chi, or African dance.

42. Plan an evening of wine, cheese, crackers, music, candles, and cozy conversation with a good friend.

43. Have your husband or significant other grease and massage your scalp.

44. See a live theater performance.

45. Enjoy a free concert in the park.

46. Take a personal retreat.

47. Get the kids to bed early and enjoy a relaxing glass of wine.

48. Rendezvous with your husband or significant other at a romantic location.

49. Buy a foam "eggshell" mattress pad. Your body will thank you.

50. Go to the zoo.

SHOW 'N' TELL

Remember the old adage "Actions speak louder than words"? As this relates to pampering and self-care my response is "Well, not always." Both actions *and* words are very important. When it comes to pampering, they actually work hand-in-hand. The actions we demonstrate and the words and language we use "show and tell" others how we want to be treated. If you respect yourself, it shows in your actions, behavior, and self-treatment. And consequently others treat you accordingly. If you are solid in your self-confidence and self-love, you won't have to keep impressing upon others that you love yourself. If you show it, act like it, exude it, and demonstrate it, others will *know* you love and respect yourself without you having to say so.

How we treat our bodies, the words we use, what we tolerate, and the value we put on our energy can all be observed by others. We literally *model* for others how we expect to be treated. As others watch us, they are in a sense being "trained." We are establishing a standard of acceptability for others' treatment of us.

So stop right now and take a step back from your life. What message are you sending others? You'll find that *others mirror back what you're projecting outward.* They tend to give back in the form of their actions and behaviors what you give to them. If you have a pattern of disrespecting others, then guess what? You'll notice that others will tend *not* to treat *you* with respect. If you constantly disregard your time, devalue your own energy, and miss appointments, then guess what? Others will mirror this back to you, *consistent* with the standards that you've demonstrated and established through your actions.

Are there areas in your life where you need to set a higher standard? What unspoken message is your appearance sending to others? Do you continue to let others' schedules, plans, and needs supersede your own? Do you easily allow your needs and plans to be bumped in order to accommodate someone else's? How and where are you using your energy?

As women we need to learn to open our mouths to let others know what we need, what works, and what doesn't work for us; what we will or won't tolerate; what we like and enjoy; and what gives us pleasure. Others are learning about our personal standards and boundaries all the time. Our personal boundaries show up in subtle ways. For example I've set up a boundary regarding phone calls during family time. We don't answer phone calls after ten P.M. on weeknights unless it's an emergency, and Sundays are reserved as Family Day. Our friends respect this.

A friend who is a consultant spends one day a week in silence and meditation. Another friend meditates every evening for thirty minutes and lets her answering machine field phone calls until she's finished. Another friend orders takeout once a week to give herself a break from cooking. Another friend treats herself to a spa facial every other month. Another friend goes to the steam room once a month to open her pores and release the toxins and impurities from her skin.

These women respect themselves and their pampering time. Their unwavering commitment to personal pampering is a testament to the value they place on their own well-being and peace of mind. In turn others mirror this behavior by respecting them and honoring their pampering time.

Authentic Support

In examining our current thoughts, beliefs, and attitudes about self-care and pampering, we must also take a look at our concept of support. As Black women we often have not received the support that we've *expected* or *needed* from the men in our lives or our children, so we've shifted and *compensated* by offloading higher *support expectations* onto our sisterfriend relationships. This happens especially when our lives are not balanced out with healthy supportive male friendships. Then we tend to overburden our sisterfriend relationships as the sole source of our emotional fulfillment. This is not altogether bad, but it can have the effect of suppressing our sisterfriendships and making them fragile beneath the surface. Often we don't vocalize these expectations. They go unspoken. Yet we get upset, hurt, or disappointed when our expectations aren't met. This starts to perpetuate an unhealthy relationship dynamic, and our close sisterfriendships start to feel heavy and draining.

In our minds our Support Expectation Equation goes something like this: If she supports me and was there for me when I had my crisis or my last round of drama, then she's down for me—she's a *real* sisterfriend. But in essence we're requiring a sisterfriend to *prove* her love for us based upon her response to *our* personal crisis. We expect a sisterfriend to drop everything and come to our aid. And if she doesn't respond the way we think she should or want her to, she goes on our shit list, at least temporarily. In *Sisters of the Yam: black women and self-recovery,* bell hooks elaborates on this tendency Black women have. "Often we wait until a crisis situation has happened when we are compelled by circumstances to seek the help of others."

We really need to rethink this expectation that we tend to hold when it comes to our sisterfriend relationships. This keeps the focus on situations, circumstances, and incidences in which hardship is the common denominator, and a sisterfriend either "passes" or "fails" the "support test." This can foster dependent relationships that are defined by the pain and hard times you've been through together, instead of being based on joy, love, celebration, and triumph.

This cycle is a setup for frustration and disappointment. Whether or not a sisterfriend is really "down" for you should take into consideration your *entire* track record together, not just hinge on her response when you are in a jam or to a personal situation you consider to be a crisis. When we approach our sisterfriendships like this, we tend to "keep track" of whether a sisterfriend was or wasn't there for us. The relationship is not based on authentic freedom and love.

It is time for us to redefine our sisterfriendships and place them in a healthier, more stable context. Otherwise they're built upon dependency and obligation, not love. I believe this is also one of the reasons that some of us "fall out" so easily and frequently with other Black women, whereas we give others a much greater range of latitude.

Because the wants and needs of each of us are varied and diverse, it makes it easier for others to give to us if we make specific requests. This eliminates the guessing game. We tend to have a warped sense of how clearly we are making our needs known. We drop hints and "clues," hoping that others will get the message.

Then, when others don't respond the way we *think* they should or the way we want them to, we get upset, claiming, "You aren't being supportive" or "I don't feel supported."

I've noticed that we tend to throw this term *support* around rather loosely. When a sisterfriend doesn't respond the way we'd like her to, we'll throw the "I don't feel that you supported me" accusation at her. Sometimes we act as if our sisterfriends have an obligation to help bail us out of the messes that *we* create.

Let me give you a little scenario. You haven't heard from one of your close sisterfriends in over a week, and it is unusual for her to go this long without touching base. You give her a call to check in. She answers the phone and you ask, "So, girl, what's been going on with you? Is everything cool?" She responds by giving you a full report blow-by-blow on the hell that's broken loose in her life. She explains that she hasn't called because she's been so busy trying to deal with all of it. You listen quietly and patiently for about twenty-five minutes as she describes the "shit" that's been happening in her life. After she finishes, you ask a few questions for clarification, then compassionately offer some heartfelt words of encouragement and some practical suggestions for her situation. You conclude the conversation by saying, "Let me know how I can help, girl," then hang up the phone.

You call back three days later to see how she's doing, and she lets you know that she is upset with you. This response comes totally out of left field and catches you off guard, and you ask, "Why?!? What for?" She explains that you knew she was going through hell, yet you were unsupportive. (Side note: A quick way to strike a chord in another sisterfriend is to tell her she's not being "support-ive." This gets a rise out of us because we are programmed and conditioned to be supportive and accommodating of others' needs. So hearing that we're *not* "supportive" disturbs our social program-ming. After all, not being supportive means not being sensitive, not being empathic, not being thoughtful. We must realize that this type of reaction is often guilt-driven.) So the end result is that she's hurt and you feel bad. These feelings don't serve either of you.

Freeze frame. Let's pause here for a moment to revisit the series of events that transpired between you and your friend. To get a fairer and more accurate picture of this situation, we'd need to see the dynamics of the *history* of the friendship as well. But for now let's focus on what transpired in these phone conversations. In the original phone conversation did your girlfriend articulate how, given her closeness to her own situation, you could best support her and be of service? Did she give you an authentic "read" on her emotional state so that you'd have a clearer sense of how best to support her, or did she give you a narrated play-by-play of the crisis? After she gave you a description of "the hell" that was break-ing loose in her life, did she balance it out by making specific re-quests for support? Did she request help, or did she expect you to "just know" what she needed?

You listened fully and could hear that things were crazy, but does that mean that you intuitively knew the most appropriate sup-port she needed given *her* situation? Not necessarily. In order to avoid the bad feelings that can come out of this type of situation, your friend could have made it easier on both of you if she had made a request for support that addressed her needs. She could have said, "Girl, I need a break. Can I bring the kids over for a couple of hours so that I can have some quiet time?" Or "I'm depressed and I need to lift my spirits. Can we go out and listen to some jazz tomorrow night?" Or "I need you to listen so that I can get some of this stuff off my chest." Any of these requests would have been helpful.

In our sisterfriend relationships we tend to talk *about* the situation, giving a blow-by-blow, narrative report of what is going on. But we don't disclose our feelings or needs, or, more important, the *type* of support that we need given the situation. We'll hold on to our internal, nonvoiced expectations, yet get upset with a sisterfriend if she doesn't intuitively or telepathically know what we need.

My point is this: We need to do a better job of straight out asking for what we need, and this applies in our love relationships too. And we don't have to be harsh and demanding about it. Knowing what you need and then asking for it to be provided is noble. When you shift to a truly self-caring lifestyle, your life will reflect more balance and less crisis and drama. This gives our sisterfriend-ships more stability and allows them room to grow in new and healthier ways.

Early on in my marriage I realized that just because I was married didn't mean that my husband, Joe, could telepathically sense all of my wants and needs. I had to open my mouth. I realized that I wanted him to bring me fresh flowers once in a while just because, not due to a holiday or special occasion. I made this request one evening, after also explaining how much I enjoyed receiving flowers from him and how good they made me feel. He listened and said he was happy to oblige me. After this brief conversation about the flowers I put it in the back of my mind. Then one evening weeks later my husband arrived home from work with a beautiful bouquet of purple irises in his hand. When I saw them, my mind raced to recall what special event I had forgotten. "Oh, honey," I said, "these are beautiful! But what's the occasion?" He replied, "The occasion is that we're both alive and well. Isn't that reason enough? And didn't you say that you wanted to receive fresh flowers when there was no special occasion?" I chuckled to myself, then answered, "Yes, you're absolutely right." I was getting what I asked for.

When I wanted to celebrate the success of the first annual Pacific Northwest African-American Women's Advance, I decided that an Empowerment Party would be a great way to include others in my celebration. But for my Empowerment Party to come about, I had to make a request to the sisterfriend that I wanted to serve as my party hostess and coordinator. If I had simply told my girlfriend that I wanted to celebrate, in *her* mind she might have decided to take me out to dinner or give me a gift. These would certainly have been nice heartfelt gestures, but the truth of the matter was that *I* had the clearest sense of what I wanted and needed. So I made a request to someone I knew had *the ability to respond to it*. After all, you wouldn't ask a person for a ride who doesn't have a car, would you?

I shared the vision for my party with her. I wanted to be surrounded by a group of my dearest sisterfriends, and I wanted the setting to feel like the royal chambers of a queen, complete with candles, music, fresh flowers, incense, and delicious food. When you make a request, it's important to give the other person the room to decline the request as well. *This is a very important component of a request.* So that it doesn't feel like pressure or obligation to the other person, it has to be made in a spirit in which either yes or no answers are okay. My girlfriend graciously accepted the request to be my hostess. To me this was authentic support: knowing what you need; asking it of someone who has the ability, means, and disposition to respond positively to it; and then having your need provided for. This is my definition of authentic support. Being able to ask for what you need isn't a sign of weakness; on the contrary it enhances your personal power.

A couple of years ago, before heading off for three days to Atlanta to conduct a seminar at the African-American Women on Tour conference, I asked my husband to throw me a Bon Voyage Party. I asked him to keep the guest list very short—just him and me. I let him know that I was leaving the details of the party up to him to do whatever he so chose, and that whatever he decided to do was okay with me. This was so that he wouldn't feel any pressure to do it *my* way. He accepted.

The night before my departure for Atlanta he called me from work to let me know that we'd need to get the girls to bed early so that we would have some quality time for the Bon Voyage Party. That evening he sent me down the hall into my office. About twenty minutes later he came to retrieve me. He told me to close my eyes and led me back into the living room by the hand. I could hear the sultry crooning of Will Downing coming from the stereo and I could smell the African Love incense burning. I opened my eyes to behold a lovely sight. My husband had turned down the lights and placed lit candles around the living room, giving it a soft romantic glow. A bottle of opened champagne and two tall-stemmed crystal champagne glasses sat on the coffee table. Beside them he had lovingly arranged a platter of luscious red grapes, cheese, and crackers. He guided me over to the couch and asked me to take a seat and get comfortable. "Wow!" I said. "Honey, this is wonderful." We nibbled on grapes, cheese, and crackers and enjoyed some cozy conversation while we sipped wine, laughed, and snuggled. After making several toasts to the success of my trip, he presented me with a sealed envelope. He told me it was a card that I was not to open until I was on the plane and up in the sky on my way to Atlanta.

The next day I waited anxiously for the plane to take off so that I could tear open the envelope. Once the plane reached its cruising altitude, I opened the envelope and read the card. I read it three times, slowly. By the end of the third reading I had tears in my eyes. I was so moved by my husband's words of love and encouragement. One of the lines he wrote in the card read, "Honey, you remind me of everything that's good in this world." My private Bon Voyage Party and my special card set the tone for what turned out to be a magnificent trip. And it happened as a result of first making a request.

PAMPERING WITH A PARTNER

This section is not only for those who are married or in committed relationships, it is also for those who are in *preparation* for their Divine Mate. Introducing partner pampering into my marriage has kept it passionate and spicy. Partner pampering reminds me that marriage is a sacred union and that my husband is a *living gift*. I am mindful that I should remain continuously grateful for him and for our union.

Just as you went through a personal process earlier getting clear with yourself about what brings you joy, a similar type of process can also be done with your partner to determine what brings the *two* of you joy, together. So the key question is modified to "What Bring *Us* Joy?" The important consideration to keep in mind with a partner is that all of the partner pampering must be done *together*, beginning with the "What Brings Us Joy" exercise. When you make out your list, be sure that it is cocreated. Release any urge to take charge and come up with the list by yourself.

You may need to help facilitate your partner-pampering activities at first in order to be sure that they happen, but generating the list should be a cooperative effort. Be aware that your partner may be a little resistant at first to the notion of partner pampering. Be patient and explain it as something fun and bonding, not something that is going to "help the relationship" or "help him open up." In the early phases of partner pampering, you may need to coax and nudge your partner along. Especially if he doesn't want to participate in making out the list. I certainly had to do some coaxing and nudging with Joe.

*   *   *

Since we both enjoy reading, I thought a partner-pampering activity related to reading would be a good place for us to start. Even though our reading interests are different—Joe enjoys reading the newspaper and magazines, while I'm a voracious book reader—the common ground was that we both enjoyed it. I already had a personal reading ritual. Every other week I would pick an evening to read. I would let Joe know in advance that I'd be retiring early to do some reading. So I thought it would be nice to start including him in this reading ritual.

One evening as I was about to retire, I asked Joe if he wanted to come into the bedroom to join me since he was sitting on the couch reading the evening newspaper anyway. He said, "Sure." About ten minutes later he came in and stretched out on the bed with me and continued reading his newspaper. I offered him a cup of tea to go along with the soft jazz and gentle bedside lamplight. Ten minutes later he glanced up from his newspaper to ask what I was reading. At the time, it was *The Isis Papers* by Dr. Frances Cres Welsing. He asked what the book was about and I gave him a quick overview of the section I was reading. He looked very intrigued, so I offered to read a few paragraphs out loud to him so that he could get a better "taste" of it. After hearing just three paragraphs of the book, his interest was piqued. He asked if he could read it after I finished with it. Without hesitation I said, "Of course."

I finished the book a few days later and, as promised, I handed it off to him. A week and a half later, when it was again time for my reading ritual, he asked if he could join me! But this time, instead of bringing his newspaper back with him, he brought *The Isis Papers*. And this was the beginning of our partner reading ritual. Outside of a few books on finance or investments, this was the first book he'd fully read since college. He admitted that he had never considered himself someone who enjoyed reading books because he had so many negative associations from school. Reading books is now an enjoyable experience for Joe, ever since I *reframed* it in the context of a special partner-pampering activity.

This partner reading ritual was created around the simple activity of reading. See how simple activities can be enhanced to a sacred level by elevating them into rituals? Let your imagination and creativity loose to explore and roam. The sky is the limit as long as you and your partner are in agreement.

Here are some other simple ideas for partner pampering:

• *Pillow talk*—Another partner pampering ritual that Joe and I do is something I call Pillow Talk. For Pillow Talk we lie down on our sides, face-to-face on our bed only about ten inches apart. We then have a cozy conversation or discuss a juicy topic. The key is to look into each other's eyes as you converse. Being this close, having an intimate conversation, and looking deeply into each other's eyes is warm and bonding. Embracing in a loose hug, intertwining your legs, or cupping each other's face while you are talking adds nicely to Pillow Talk.

• *Foot massages*—Once a month we have foot-massage night. One month it's his turn to receive, and the next month it's mine. You first soak your feet for about five minutes in a basin of warm water scented with a couple drops of essential oils such as jasmine, lavender, or eucalyptus. The lavender and jasmine have natural relaxation properties, and the eucalyptus has natural revitalizing qualities. Then we use our vanilla or strawberry massage balm, or our homemade Egyptian musk–scented massage oil to rub into the other's feet.

• *Friday-night dates*—Friday night is our standing at-home video night together. If either of us makes plans with friends, we try to make it on Saturday nights so as not to interfere with our standing Friday-night "date" with each other. I usually cook four nights a week, but on Friday nights I don't cook. We'll pick up some takeout Chinese food or order in a pizza. We get the girls to bed early, then we cuddle up on the couch and enjoy Breyer's vanilla bean ice cream while we watch a good video.

• *Indoor picnic*—One time I decided to try something a little different with dinner. As usual I planned for dinner to be ready when my husband got home from work. But this time I decided to set it up picnic-style, in the middle of the living room on a blanket. When my husband came in the door, he was greeted by a picnic spread, complete with paper plates and plastic forks and spoons. I had even managed to dig out a bottle of wine that had been tucked away in the back of the refrigerator. We sat down on the floor and enjoyed a delicious picnic dinner.

• *The Discovery Game*—Another partner pampering activity we like to do once in a while is a little game I made up called the Discovery Game. The object of the game is to have fun discovering new things about your partner from a set of simple questions that you each make up. We like to play the game sitting up in bed. This is how it works. You each need a piece of paper and a pen or pencil. Make three even columns on your paper. Leaving space between, write the numbers one through seven down the left side of the paper. Give yourselves five minutes for each of you to come up with a set of seven simple but fun questions that you think will reveal unknown aspects of the other's character. Write your seven questions in the first column. For example one of the questions my husband put down on his list was, "If you could go on a cruise with anyone in the world, past or present, male or female, who would it be?" In the second column take five minutes to write down what you each *think* your partner's answer to the question will be. Then you each ask the seven questions of the other partner and record the answers. Lastly have fun seeing who got the most "right" about the other. The first time we played, my husband got more correct about me than I did about him, much to my amazement.

• *Love letters*—To add a little pampering flair to our Valentine's Day, we've started writing love letters to read and exchange over dinner. We each take a turn reading our love letter to the other. My Valentine's Day love letters are special keepsakes I cherish and keep in my Wish Box on my altar.

• *Slow dancing*—We slow-dance together in the living room. Since Joe likes Anita Baker and I like Luther Vandross, we slow-dance to a song from each of them.

• *Mini-getaways*—As an inexpensive alternative to an out-of-town getaway, we arrange to stay at one of the local bed and breakfasts (B&B). The first time we did this, we selected a B&B that was a turn-of-the-century mansion, complete with a parlor, library, fireplace, hearty antique furniture, crystal chandeliers, and polished oak banisters along the stairway. Though we were still in Seattle, as soon as we set foot inside the B&B, we felt as if we'd been transported to Chicago or San Francisco in the early 1900s.

THE RIPPLE EFFECT

One of the most rewarding outcomes of shifting to a self-caring lifestyle is seeing it "rub off" on others. One evening I was pleasantly surprised when my husband came home from work and informed me that he planned to retire early for the evening to pamper himself. He asked if I could get the girls squared away for the evening so that he could do this. Of course I agreed. An hour later I decided to go and check on him to see how he was doing. (Actually I was being nosy.) He was in the bathroom, so I knocked on the door and asked if it was okay for me to come in. He said yes. I walked into the bathroom to find my husband submerged in a bubble bath, kicked back with his head resting on my bath pillow, listening to jazz, and reading his *Men's Health* magazine. He looked up and said, "Good timing, honey. Would you please bring me a glass of ice water?" I jokingly replied with my best mock British accent, "Most certainly, sir," and came back with his ice water. Seeing my husband indulging in a bubble bath was clear evidence to me that pampering has a ripple effect. It expands to affect others in your life in positive ways.

One of my girlfriends collects African instruments. And a few years ago she hosted a Pampering Party in honor of another one of our girlfriends and her teenage daughter. Near the end of the party I suggested that we each grab an instrument and have a spontaneous, homemade concert. We sat in a circle with drums, xylophones, rattles, finger pianos, and wooden flutes. I suggested that we start with a drum beat and then add in each additional instrument one by one until everyone was playing. The grand finale of our homespun concert was adding the singing. So that we would each have a turn leading, we went around the circle ad-libbing chants call-and-response style. We were jamming! I'm sure my girl-friend's neighbors were wondering what we crazy Black women were doing in her apartment with all of the laughter, whooping, hollering, singing, and playing.

7

THE NEW YOU

My goal in writing this book has been to help you discover a new way of living, a new way of being, and a new approach to life in which pampering is a healthy priority. My hope is that you're on your way to embracing a new empowering perspective that is focused on self-care as healthy self-service. The journey to the place where pampering is *integrated* into the very fiber of your life is not without its bumps along the way, but it's well worth the trip.

Keep looking for ways to pamper yourself. The possibilities are endless. After moving through this entire process I've learned some valuable lessons. I've come to realize that a self-caring attitude is not only about pampering myself. It also means obeying my intuition, honoring my truth, and being true to my vision and purpose.

THE PROOF OF THE PUDDING . . .

Through my ongoing workshops and seminars I have a chance to stay tuned in to the visible changes participants experience as they make the shift to a self-caring lifestyle. The more general results include weight release, a positive "overhaul" in personal appearance, and a more relaxed and peaceful disposition. I'd like to share a few actual case histories with you (with names changed, of course) to give you a sampling of the types of positive results I've observed:

Mariella was a single parent of two. She worked two part-time jobs, volunteered part-time with several community projects, and hosted and produced a positive talk show on a local cable channel.

We met when she was interviewing me for her local cable TV talk show. The topic was "Pampering and Self-care." After she finished the taping, she shared some of her personal story with me and asked me about the process of how to bring more balance into her life. From the information I shared during the interview taping, she realized that she hadn't made any room in her life for personal pampering. By the end of our forty-five-minute conversation she had asserted a new commitment to simplifying her life and incorporating more activities and experiences that brought her joy and pleasure. She realized that she was out tending to everyone else's needs before first seeing to her own. She was clear that the way she currently lived her life was running her ragged and that things had to change.

I saw Mariella again, four months later, when she attended one of my seminars. She looked like a different woman. Instead of the slightly frazzled and rushed look that she had had at the TV show taping, she now looked "polished" and relaxed even though she had on a sweatsuit and not a dress and nylons, as she had at the taping. The energy that surrounded her was much calmer. She was radiant. Her skin looked clearer. Her hair looked healthier, and she had re-

leased weight. I hugged her with an amazed, wide-eyed look on my face as she approached me after the seminar. "Wow!" I said. "You look fabulous. What's been going on with you?" She replied with a big smile, "I took our conversation to heart four months ago. I've started pampering myself and orienting my life more around what brings me joy. I quit my second job. I cut back on some of my community activities and I've started my morning walking routine again. I'm pursuing my singing and songwriting again, and I'm working on expanding my talk show. I've been able to spend more quality time with my daughters too. And somehow, miraculously, I'm still managing to pay all my bills!"

Then there was Danita. When I first met Danita, she was program coordinator at a local community college and had been married five years. We first met when she asked me to do a seminar for the campus women's program she coordinated. She decided to stay and sit in on my self-care and pampering workshop. After the workshop she told me how much the workshop had affected her. As she walked me out to my car, she said that it had confirmed her thoughts about needing to make some changes in her life. She had received the "kick in the butt" that she needed to get into action about them.

I saw Danita again a year later when I returned to campus to do a Healthy Love Relationships workshop. As soon as I laid eyes on her again, I could see that there had been transformation in her life. She had changed to a new hairstyle from the "curl" she'd worn for years. She was wearing a colorful, form-fitting dress and a radiant smile. She looked as if she had released about ten pounds. Her skin was glowing. Her eyes were sparkling.

She updated me on the happenings in her life. In the year since our first conversation she had finally filed for divorce after having allowed her marriage to "limp along" for several years. She had received a promotion, joined a Black women's investment club, and taken her first solo vacation. She no longer stayed at the office every night working late. She was learning to say no to accepting multiple work assignments and projects that overextended her and stressed her out. She had put her foot down and started saying "That doesn't work for me" more often. And as a result others were now respecting her boundaries and her time and energy. She was happy, very, very happy.

The Proof of the Pudding is about arriving at the phase of the process where you see the results of your transition "on the court," so to speak, and showing up as *real* in your life. What assists you in arriving at this point is the ability to keep living out of a new context, a new framework, and the persistence in *practicing and living* the sacred pampering principles.

Your transformation is now in your hands. Actually it always was. *Sacred Pampering Principles* has provided you with the tools, the coaching, and some prescriptions for achieving and maintaining a self-caring lifestyle. Whether or not it happens is up to you.

Here is a sampling of some of the types of real results and outcomes you can expect to experience if you put forth the effort and do the mental, emotional, physical, and spiritual work. The list has been compiled from my own life as well as the lives of seminar and workshop participants from over the past few years.

- More energy
- More patience, especially with your children
- Improvement in your complexion
- Feeling more in control of your life
- Gradual weight release with less effort and struggle
- A more "polished" appearance
- More radiance and glow
- Change in hairstyle
- Wearing brighter colors or more flattering clothes in general
- On time more
- Increased focus and productivity
- New clarity about your life purpose and mission
- Starting to do your life's work
- New types of female relationships
- Healthier romantic relationships
- More male friendships

- Greater willingness to try new things and take more risks
- More calm, peaceful, and centered
- Bad habits decrease
- Interpersonal relationships improve
- You smile more
- You're not as defensive
- You rediscover hobbies that have been on the back burner
- You're a better listener
- You're more decisive
- More movement activity in your life
- Sounder sleep
- Improved sex life
- Less muscle tension and body aches
- Less sickness and dis-ease
- More passionate and self-expressed
- Improved "body esteem"
- Pray and meditate more
- Increased intimacy in marriage
- Increased faith

THE PAMPERED WOMAN'S CREED

Whether all of these results become realities for you depends on practice and application of the principles. Integrating pampering into your life is a combined result of diligent practice and making healthy, self-supporting choices *ongoingly*. You've got to apply them. Hopefully you have been propelled to a higher place in your personal and feminine development, to being a universal woman who embodies love and balance.

In the back of the book I've provided you with some empowerment and pampering products to support you in achieving and sustaining a self-caring lifestyle—necessary tools for necessary maintenance. And the Pampered Woman's Creed is also provided as a tool to serve and assist you in your journey. Photocopy it and post it as a reminder of your commitment to balance and to personal well-being. It was created to

1. Give you a visual summary of powerful, self-caring affirmations
2. Remind you of the freedom of choice that exists in every moment
3. Remind you that you are a lovely w.i.p.—woman-in-process and a work-in-progress
4. Serve as a personal manifesto—your declaration of transcendence

The Pampered Woman's Creed

I am valuable.
I am worthy of being pampered.
I am one-of-a-kind,
unique in all the world
past, present, and future.
I give myself permission to put my self-care needs first.
I give myself permission to make requests of others.

I have healthy sisterfriendships based on love and stability,
not dependency, pressure, and crisis.
I give myself permission to experience joy, passion, and pleasure.
I understand that self-care and inner renewal are essential
to my mental, emotional, physical,
and spiritual well-being.
I release myself from feelings of guilt.
I forgive those who do not wish to support me.
I love me.
I deserve the very best.
I love me.
Others support me in my personal pampering plans.
My pampering plans are a priority.
I love me.
I am committed to creating a balanced lifestyle.
I create sacred spaces and places in my life.
I understand that when I take care of me first,
others are able to be better taken care of in the process.
I remind myself often that loving me does
not take away from loving others, it adds to it.
I love me.
Loving self is a prerequisite to being able
to give love away.
Love multiplies.
I can only give away that which I've developed in myself.
    I LOVE ME!

EPILOGUE

I have a vision that I'm upholding for all women, and especially Black women. I see vibrant, pampered, healed, healthy, full-filled women living balanced lives; loving others easily; being loved abundantly; and *having it all while having a ball with ease and grace*! After all, life is really about creating joy-full moments. Living life *full out*, with no regrets about what "shoulda" or "coulda" been done if we had our lives to live over.

If I Had My Life to Live Over

I'd dare to make more mistakes next time.
I'd relax, I would limber up. I would be sillier than I have been this trip. I would take fewer things seriously. I would take more chances, I would climb more mountains and swim more rivers. I would eat more ice cream and less beans. I would perhaps have more actual troubles, but I'd have fewer imaginary ones.

You see, I'm one of those people who lived sensibly and sanely hour after hour, day after day.

Oh, I've had my moments, and if I had it to do over again,
I'd have more of them. In fact, I'd try to have nothing else.

Just moments, one after another, instead of living so many years ahead of each day. I've been one of those persons who never goes anywhere without a thermometer, a hot water bottle, a raincoat and a parachute. If I had to do it again, I would travel lighter than I have.

If I had my life to live over, I would start barefoot earlier in the spring and stay that way later in the fall.
I would go to more dances. I would ride more merry-go-rounds.
I would pick more daisies.

by Nadine Stair

P.S. . . . Oh, . . . and I'd pamper myself more.

To contact Debrena Jackson Gandy about speaking engagements, keynotes, seminars, and retreats, please call 206-878-8163, fax 206-824-8973.

Do you want to be added to the Sacred Pampering Principles mailing list? Or do you have a testimony to share about how this book has affected your life? Send your name, address, testimony, and phone number to: Masterminds, 22810 30th Avenue South, Suite C101, Seattle, WA 98198.

AFROSCENTRICS® PAMPERING PRODUCTS

Item Number	Item Description	Investment
EP-01	Passionfruit Shea–Coconut Body Butter, jar	$12.50
EP-02	Passionfruit Epsom Salts for the Bath, packet	$ 4.00
EP-03	Rhythms Scented Extra-Rich Body Lotion, 4 oz., check your choice(s) ____ *Egyptian Musk* ____ *Somali Rose* ____ *Passionfruit*	$ 5.75
EP-04	Rhythms Blended Perfume Oils, ¼ oz., check your choice(s) ____ *No. 1-Passion* ____ *No. 2-Collective Healing* ____ *No. 3-Royalty* ____ *No. 4-Grace & Femininity*____ *No. 5-Exotic* ____ *No. 6-Sensuality*	$ 8.50
EP-05	Incense Sticks, 15 per packet, check your choice(s) ____*Egyptian Musk* ____ *Love* ____ *Jasmine*____ *Sandalwood*	$ 2.50
EP-06	Personal Affirmation Cards Set, 12 cards/set	$ 5.00
EP-07	Altar Cards Set, 12 cards/set	$ 7.00
EP-08	Ethnic Mini-journal & matching pen	$15.00
EP-09	Do-Not-Disturb Doorknob Sign, laminated	$ 3.00
EP-10	Pure Therapeutic Essential Oils, 1/2 oz. size	
	EP-101 Sweet Orange	$ 8.50
	EP-102 Wild Lavender	$12.00
	EP-103 Tangerine	$ 8.50
	EP-104 Grapefruit	$ 8.50
	EP-105 Wild Eucalyptus	$ 8.50
	EP-106 Wild Ylang-ylang	$26.00
EP-11	Egyptian Musk Soap	$ 4.00

Products are shipped in a reusable box. Please allow 3–4 weeks for delivery.

ORDER FORM FOR AFROSCENTRICS®
PAMPERING PRODUCTS

Name _____ Street Address _____

City/State/Zip Code _____ Phone Number _____

Item Number	Quantity	Description	Unit Price	Item Total
1.				
2.				
3.				
4.				
5.				
6.				
7.				

PRODUCTS TOTAL: $_____

Washington State residents, add sales tax: (8.2%) $_____

Subtotal: $_____

Shipping: $_____4.00

Order grand total: $_____

SEND A CHECK OR MONEY ORDER TO: AFROSCENTRICS®, 22810 30TH AVENUE SOUTH, SUITE C101, SEATTLE WA 98198. RETURNED CHECK FEE, $20.00. NO CREDIT CARDS ACCEPTED.

Please allow 3–4 weeks for delivery. Thank you.